LEADERSHIP
TRUTH
BOMBS

WHAT YOUR TEAM WANTS YOU TO KNOW BUT ISN'T TELLING YOU

LEADERSHIP
TRUTH
BOMBS

**WHAT YOUR TEAM WANTS YOU
TO KNOW BUT ISN'T TELLING YOU**

INDIE BOLLMAN

Niche Pressworks
Indianapolis, IN

Author Photograph by: Chad Dennis Photography, Inc.

Published by Niche Pressworks; NichePressworks.com
Indianapolis, IN

ISBN
Hardback: 978-1-962956-48-2
Paperback: 978-1-962956-49-9
eBook: 978-1-962956-50-5

Library of Congress Cataloging-in-Publication Data on File at lccn.loc.gov

WHAT OTHERS ARE SAYING

I have known Indie personally and professionally for over 15 years. *Leadership Truth Bombs* is a culmination of her time in the trenches and highlights her true passion for building teams and inspiring leaders. Indie hits a home run, presenting the Truth Bomb concepts in a clear, concise, and real-world approach. From the opening pages to the last chapter, this book is a must-read for new leaders as well as seasoned professionals and has something for everyone. We are all leaders in some way, whether leading business teams or leading our families. These are approaches that will apply in any leadership environment. I can't wait to read *Leadership Truth Bombs 2.0*!

— **CHRISS SPIRES,** partner, The Baldwin Group

Leadership Truth Bombs hits you with the truths your team wishes you knew and won't say. It's a bold, no-nonsense guide to leading with heart, purpose, and authenticity. If you're ready to transform your leadership and inspire your team, this book is a must-read!

— **HERNANI ALVES,** author of *Balanced Accountability: Create a Culture of Ownership* and *The Champion Advantage: Winning with Change*

At a time when employee morale and workplace productivity are at an all-time low, this is the perfect read for any leader — no matter where they are in their career. I have known Indie personally for almost a decade and have seen the love and enthusiasm she pours into her teams, as well as her ability to turn any team into high-performing "rock stars" by using this methodology. Indie's straightforward approach helps us face the uncomfortable truths of the complex world of leadership and understand how to be the leaders that everyone — including ourselves — wants us to be. I wish I had had this book when I first started in leadership!

— **HARRISON PACIOTTI,** sales executive, major accounts, ADP

WANT MORE?

I've got you covered!

Go to my bonus content page on my website, where you can:

- Download **bonus Leadership Truth Bombs**
- Sign up for my **monthly newsletter with ideas, thoughts, and methods** to support you and your team
- Follow me on my social channels!

www.indiebollman.com/ltbbonus

To all the teams I've had the honor to serve.
Thank you for teaching me
and for all the joy I got from watching you grow.

ACKNOWLEDGEMENTS

It would be wrong of me if I didn't give a shout-out to a few folks who have inspired me along the way, and so I will.

They deserve it, along with my heartfelt thanks. The forever kind.

The first is, undoubtedly, my dad. He was old-school in that "greatest generation" way.

He taught me a few things that I try hard to live up to every day. "Do the right thing" was one, along with "Do your job better than anyone else has." There were others, of course, but these two have stuck with me the most. Daddy, if you can hear me, I didn't forget what you taught me. I hope you see some of your lessons come through in how I live my life and in the pages of this book. I listened to every word. And I miss you.

Then there's Chriss Spires. I met Chriss 15 or so years ago through another one of my amazing friends. Chriss is, in his own right, a very successful and accomplished businessman, and he gets my respect in big doses from that alone.

He's also an incredible friend.

Chriss, I sure hope you know how much I appreciate your friendship and support while I've walked into this new chapter of my life; your support has helped me move forward in what I can and want to do and how I can give back to others doing it. I wasn't sure I could do it until you convinced me otherwise. I know I've said thank you a gazillion times, but it doesn't seem nearly enough. I'll just have to say it a gazillion more, and maybe a few more times after that.

I'd be horribly remiss if I didn't mention two other friends: the one, the only, amazing best-selling author Steve Farber and his wonderful wife, Veronica. Steve, your work and your life have inspired me to do more, do it better, and always bring love into the nine-to-five. I had no idea how much I would need to rely on these things in the years after we first met. Your writing and the example you and Veronica live each day have meant so much to me. I'll never forget it. Not ever. Big love, my friends.

And next, my sister, Sandie. Man, has she ever stood by me, stood up for me as only a big sister can, and listened to my stories over and over (and sometimes over again) through the years, far beyond what other friends were prepared to do. Sis, I literally wouldn't have made it without you, and hope that you know I am here for you just as you have been for me. Always.

Thanks also to my daughter, Jess, and my granddaughter, Drew. They are my world. They inspire me each day, Jess with her amazing intelligence and ability to drive through the toughest of times to get things done, and Drew with her curious mind and fresh eyes on the world and everything in it. I try to see all things these days through Drew's beautiful lens of innocence — loving her has changed me forever and continues to remind me of how much I am able to love, and feel loved, every day. Yep, I'm one lucky mom and grammy.

Last and, yes, I'm gonna go there: I thank my Creator. Pretty sure I'd be lost without Him. God's strength guides me even when He has to shove me hard to get my attention — but I'm listening, Big Guy. I am grateful every day for His love, healing, and reminders that He's there beside me through all things and that He loves me.

He loves you too, by the way.

TABLE OF CONTENTS

What Others Are Saying   v
Acknowledgements   xi
Foreword: An Invitation to Be the Leader Your Team Deserves xv
Introduction: The Mother of All Truth Bombs   1

TRUTH BOMB # 1   It's All Personal, Every Bit of It   9
TRUTH BOMB # 2   There Are No Brilliant Jerks on
                     a Dream Team   23
TRUTH BOMB # 3   You Can't Cherry-Pick Who to Be Kind To   35
TRUTH BOMB # 4   Don't Lose Your Sh*t   45
TRUTH BOMB # 5   Beware of FIFB   55
TRUTH BOMB # 6   Cliques Suck   65
TRUTH BOMB # 7   Don't Call Them Family Unless
                     You Mean It   77
TRUTH BOMB # 8   If You Show People You Do or Don't
                     Care, They'll Return the Favor   89
TRUTH BOMB # 9   Hire Great People, Then Get Out of
                     Their Way   103
TRUTH BOMB # 10 You Have a Minute   113
TRUTH BOMB # 11 It's About Their Growth, Not Yours   123
TRUTH BOMB # 12 How You Treat (and Teach) Your
                     Employees = How Your Customers
                     Are Treated   137
TRUTH BOMB # 13 How Great a Leader You Are Is Up to You   147
TRUTH BOMB # 14 If You Want People to Work with Their
                     Hearts, You Have to Lead with Yours   157

Epilogue: Thank You, Derrick   167
Endnotes   171
About the Author   175

AN INVITATION TO BE THE LEADER YOUR TEAM DESERVES

A particular kind of magic happens when someone moves from student to teacher — when they take what they've learned, blend it with their own hard-won wisdom, and create something entirely new that helps others transform their own lives and work. That's exactly what Indie Bollman has done with this remarkable book.

I first met Indie when she attended one of my Extreme Leadership workshops several years ago. From our very first interaction, I could tell she was different. While others were taking notes, Indie was making connections. While others were learning concepts, she was already thinking about application. She wasn't just absorbing the material — she was extending it, challenging it, living it.

That's why I wasn't surprised when she went on to become one of our most impactful certified trainers at the Extreme Leadership Institute. Indie has that rare ability to take complex leadership principles and make them both accessible and actionable. But more important, she embodies what she teaches. She leads with love — yes, I said love.

Which brings us to this book you're holding. *Leadership Truth Bombs*® is exactly what the title promises: direct, sometimes uncomfortable, but absolutely essential truths about what it really takes to lead people effectively. These aren't theoretical concepts developed in some ivory tower. These are hard-earned insights from someone who has been in the trenches, who has made the mistakes, celebrated the victories, and learned the lessons that only come from doing the work.

What I particularly appreciate about Indie's approach is how she weaves together the personal and professional aspects of leadership. Too often, we try to separate these as if we're different people at work than we are at home. But as Indie powerfully demonstrates, great leadership is fundamentally about being human — about bringing your whole self to work and creating environments where others can do the same.

Take her first Truth Bomb, for instance: "It's All Personal, Every Bit of It." In just those seven words, she challenges one of the most persistent and damaging myths in business — the idea that we can somehow separate the personal from the professional. As Indie shows us, not only is this impossible, but it's also not even desirable. When we try to pretend that business isn't personal, we strip away the very things that make great leadership possible: empathy, connection, and, yes, love.

This book is full of similar insights, each one challenging conventional wisdom while offering a more human, more effective way forward. Whether she's talking about the dangers of "brilliant jerks" (there's no place for them on a dream team), the importance of leading with heart, or why you can't cherry-pick who to be kind to, Indie cuts through the noise and gets to what really matters in leadership.

What makes these Truth Bombs particularly powerful is that they're not just observations — they're invitations. Each one challenges you to examine your own leadership style, to question your assumptions, and to consider how you might show up differently for your team. And Indie guides you through this process with the perfect blend of challenge and support, pushing you to be better while acknowledging that we're all works in progress.

I've spent my career studying and teaching about Extreme Leadership — about what it takes to create extraordinary re-sults while developing and inspiring others. And I can tell you that what Indie has created here isn't just another leadership book. It's a manifesto for a more human, more effective way of leading. It's a guide for those who want to make a real dif-ference in the lives of the people they lead while driving excep-tional business results.

Whether you're a seasoned executive, a new manager, or someone who aspires to lead oth-ers, you'll find valuable insights and practical wisdom in these pages. But be warned: These Truth Bombs will challenge you.

> **What Indie has created here isn't just another leadership book. It's a manifesto for a more human, more effective way of leading.**

They'll make you uncomfortable at times. They'll force you to confront some hard truths about yourself and your leadership style. And that's exactly why they work.

In a world that desperately needs better leaders — leaders who can build trust, inspire innovation, and create environments where people can do their best work — Indie's voice is both timely and essential. She reminds us that great leadership isn't about having all the answers or being perfect. It's about being real, being human, and being willing to do the hard work of helping others become the best versions of themselves.

Read this book. Let these Truth Bombs detonate in your consciousness. And then use what you learn to become the kind of leader your people deserve and your organization needs.

— **STEVE FARBER,** President, Extreme Leadership, Inc., and CEO and founder of The Extreme Leadership Institute; best-selling author of *The Radical Leap, The Radical Edge, Greater Than Yourself,* and *Love Is Just Damn Good Business*

THE MOTHER OF ALL TRUTH BOMBS

Before we go any further into this book, there's a story I'd like to share with you. It's an important one, because it's *THE* story that started all this Truth Bomb talk for me. It's not from anything recent, and it's not even my story. But it had a big impression on me, and from the day I heard it, I began paying close attention to the impact that leaders have on their teams.

It's about a close friend of mine who was an administrative assistant many years ago at a consulting firm. We'll call him Derrick because I like that name. Anyway, Derrick and I were on the phone catching up, and I could tell he was upset.

"What's wrong?" I asked.

"I'm upset about something that happened today," he replied.

"What happened?" I asked, concerned. It wasn't like Derrick to let things get to him, so I could tell this was something out of the ordinary.

He told me the story, which went something like this.

Derrick was trying to get some work done when he heard a muffled conversation coming from his boss's office, the door of which was close to Derrick's desk.

"What?" his boss exclaimed, so loudly that Derrick stopped what he was doing. Hearing the irritation in her voice, he wondered what on earth could be wrong.

"For *some* reason my new client was *not* allowed to register today for the upcoming event," said the sales executive on the other end of the call with Derrick's boss. The man wasn't even on speaker; he was just so ticked off and loud that Derrick could hear him anyway. "He was told he missed the deadline!"

Derrick's shoulders tensed. This didn't sound good at all.

"Are you *kidding* me?" his boss replied, matching the tone and volume of the sales executive on the other end of the line, and then added, "These *assholes* up here don't know what they're doing."

Derrick swallowed, his mind racing as he tried to figure out what was happening. *Wait, what? Assholes?*

Then he began to understand what they were talking about. The deadline they were referring to was related to an upcoming event they were hosting. The boss had told everyone just the week before that the deadline was final, and no registrations were to be accepted after it passed — none whatsoever.

When Derrick realized this, his heart sank. *That's* me she's *referring to,* he suddenly thought. *I'm the only one who the client would have talked to. I would have been the one who told him he had missed the deadline. I'm the one she's calling an asshole.*

Even though he thought he understood the conversation, however, it still didn't make any sense. *Why is she angry about me enforcing the deadline she set?* he wondered, mystified. He could feel his face turning red hot with embarrassment and shock.

After the call ended, still feeling the sting of being called an asshole by his boss, Derrick kept replaying her conversation word for word through his head, questioning whether he had messed up.

He quickly checked the memo. Had he heard the directions about the deadline wrong?

Nope. The date was right there, along with the instructions not to let anyone else register after it. It was all clear as day. He had done exactly as he'd been told to do. In fact, he prided himself on getting the instructions right and following them correctly.

Nothing made sense. *I've always had such a great relationship with and admired my boss,* he thought. *Surely she wouldn't call me that. Not like that, and not to others.*

But it still hung there, the word "assholes." He played that part over in his mind again, feeling a sense of dread, which was immediately followed by the horrible feeling of hurt. This was someone he looked up to and had loyally served. She had chosen to call him a name just to appease someone else instead of standing up for him. It was suddenly clear to Derrick that his boss was capable of saying anything — even something untrue or disrespectful — to solve a situation.

"It's all just wrong, and *so* unfair," Derrick said to me. "I've been emotionally messed up all day. I'll never trust her again, and I'll never give my all again — not *ever*. I wonder how many times she has done this before and about who. They'd be crushed." He wondered whether he should warn the others on her team.

Trust was gone, and loyalty was right on its heels.

I still remember that story as vividly as if Derrick had told it to me five minutes ago. His boss may have long forgotten it, but Derrick never did.

I didn't either.

I wasn't yet a leader at the time, but the story taught me a big lesson about leadership and made me think long and hard about my own experience with leaders and leading a team myself. It put me on a path of paying close attention to leadership behavior and how teams feel about certain things.

It's a clear example showing that what a leader does and says can impact their team in a big way, and that impact can last for a very, *very* long time.

When you are a leader, your team notices all of these things. And yet, they may or may not *tell* you these things, these truths, as I like to refer to them. Whether the feedback is well founded or not, they, like Derrick, may not feel safe saying it to you. Safety is an important topic, and it's one we'll talk about more later in the book.

To make the situation even worse, situations like Derrick's can affect not only those directly involved, but everyone else who hears it or hears about it. When someone is upset, they will likely tell others if only to spare them. Derrick told me, after all, and here I am writing about it today. It's kind of the gift that keeps on giving, and not in a good way. Who knows how many other teammates he told? And who knows how many they told as well?

So, even though you may not realize there are any issues, that doesn't mean there aren't any underlying problems affecting you as a leader. The effect can come across as a feeling of disconnect from your team, or maybe you get a sense that they aren't engaged or motivated by what they're doing in their role.

You need to know these things, no matter who tells you.

So I'm going to share what they won't, in the hope that it will enable you to understand your team more, feel more connected to them, and help them have a genuine sense of excitement about what they do and about your seeing their value. And as a wonderful bonus, you may find a new way to lead them to their full potential.

LEADERSHIP TRUTH BOMBS ARE BORN

I remember when the idea of calling these lessons the Leadership Truth Bombs® bounced into my head. I was with a company where we had worked hard to transform the culture over several years. One of the first things I'd done shortly after joining them was to build out an internal leadership development program to establish and support a strong leadership philosophy. We wanted to transform the culture to one that would help the employees and the company grow. We wanted it to be a place where the employees felt valued and appreciated, where they felt free to create and innovate while focusing on how we served others. And that is exactly what we did.

One day before beginning a session of the leadership development program, I was online and saw a picture of an enormous wave. Wouldn't you know it — it's referred to in surfing circles as a "bomb" wave. Now, I'm not in the surfing circles, mind you, given *Jaws*[1] and all that. So this kind of wave isn't something you'd ever find me riding on (or any other kind of wave, for that matter), but a light bulb went off just the same.

You see, I think the truth is like that big ol' wave. Big, even scary at times. But there it is — undeniable, washing over you and knocking you around a bit. You can try to ignore it, but here it comes anyway.

Just like that wave, the truth is relentless. It will knock you around a bit until you acknowledge it, and if you don't, well, here it comes again (and again).

Right after that bomb wave realization hit me, I began gathering and organizing the things I had noted through the years about what teams really want from their leaders. They are truths I've learned throughout my career. They are simple, and aren't always sugarcoated — just like the truth, right? And like those big bomb waves, they knock us around now and then, until we see their value and the firm footing understanding them can provide.

Throughout the years as my career grew and I was in more leadership positions, I learned that teams just assume their leaders already know, or *should* know, these things. When leaders don't, their teams may be a little afraid to correct them. Then the leader never gets a chance to get better, and that's not fair to anyone.

This book is meant to give leaders — including you — that chance. I truly believe that our workplaces can bring real joy into the lives of our teams, and it starts with how we lead those we are responsible for. I want you to know what I've learned through my years of feeling, watching, and understanding these things from my own experience and from the phenomenal teams that I had the honor to lead. I hope to fill some of that knowledge gap in hopes of giving you that chance to change things for the better.

Your main obligation as a leader, the biggest one in my opinion, is helping your team grow. You simply must drop the need to be in the limelight and must put your team in it instead. There's a place for ego in leadership, mind you, but it's lightly sprinkled only here and there and only when absolutely needed. It should never be the priority when you're guiding a team. More on this later too.

It's important for you to know these things because, while our team members don't always tell us what they want from us, I can tell you with 100 percent certainty they want to.

Your team wants you to know what they need from you.

Our teams also want a better workplace, and they want to help their leaders do a better job to create that. They long to feel they are a part of something wonderful and to understand their part in the overall purpose of the organization.

The bottom line is, they want to work from their hearts.

The trick is, we must lead with our own hearts for that to happen. (Spoiler alert: There's a Truth Bomb devoted to this later in the book. Stay tuned.)

I share the Truth Bombs that follow in hopes that they will help you create the kind of workplace I know is possible.

And it *is* possible. You can create it by finding and keeping the kind of talent you need for your business, by leading them well now and in the future, and by teaching them to be great leaders too.

And with that comes a quick reminder: Keep in mind the type of new leaders you want to develop to keep a good thing like this going. If you want your business to keep growing, you need to get clear on how those leaders are treating your folks, as well as what values they bring in each day with them. More on that later too.

As you read, grab onto the Truth Bombs that ring true, and *especially* grab the ones that tick you off a little — chances are those are the truest and the ones you'll grow from.

The rest, well, just keep them in mind or pay it forward by helping other leaders learn from them too.

One more thing: The names and dates in the stories I use in the book have been changed, but the general circumstances and feelings around them have not.

Now: Ready to talk truths?

Me too.

Let's get started, why don't we?

CHAPTER ONE

IT'S ALL PERSONAL, EVERY BIT OF IT

"It's not personal... it's just business."

We've all heard it, right? Heck, we've probably all *said* it.

No one feels good when they hear it, though. That's because it's usually followed by some crappy news. It's almost always a disclaimer that some people use to give themselves permission to give the crappy news.

Of course, this may mean they know the crappy news is something the receiver can't help but take personally.

IT'S ALSO HURTFUL

I cover this Leadership Truth Bomb first because it's foundational to everything else in the book. For me, it's the one to always keep in mind in leading and in learning to be better at it for your team.

Trying to placate someone by letting yourself off the hook with "it's not personal, it's just business" doesn't lessen the impact on them; in fact, it makes it worse.

I've unfortunately had to sit in on meetings where an employee was being terminated. These are some of the saddest memories of my career, and something no leader ever looks forward to. Many of these meetings were the result of economic issues. The company had to make changes to stay afloat, and those changes had nothing to do with the employee's performance.

But, as much as that was obvious to everyone involved, I can tell you with certainty that when the employee was legitimately told, "It's not personal, it's just a business decision," not once did they smile and say, "Hey, no problemo, it's all good." Instead, 100 percent of the time, they took it *very* personally.

They were, in that instant, wondering what happened, what they did wrong (even if the decision was not performance related), what they should have done differently, etc. Also, they were wondering how the *heck* they were going to pay their bills in the coming weeks.

I read an article recently where the author suggested that trying to *not* take work personally is an "absurd" idea.[2] He's right.

He added the reason is that most of our waking hours are spent in our workplace, making it nearly impossible to *not* take it personally.

He's right about that too, and he's not alone in that opinion.

A quick search on the internet will result in articles, posts, and blogs where business leaders, employees, and others have chimed in on the subject — that business is *very* personal. One LinkedIn post I read reminded leaders that each employee is a dad, mom, son, or daughter who depends on their job to support themselves and their families. The author went on to sum it up nicely with "it's not business, it's *personal.*"

Rick Lenz, co-founder of TAG Group Holdings, is another example. He's quoted right on his company's web page: "*All* business is personal, and the very best business is very personal."[3]

Go, Rick.

It's easy to understand the personal nature of work for employees, once you consider the time and effort they spend at work with teammates. They form relationships and friendships in the workplace that may last far beyond their time there. In addition, companies generally want people to be engaged in what they are doing, buying into what the company stands for and what they are selling.

Those things are *all* personal.

Suddenly dismissing that by prefacing bad news with the "it's not personal" line is equal to suddenly treating them very *im*personally. And at a time when it counts the most.

Because they're people — they feel things.

You do too.

IT'S A BIT MANIPULATIVE

The "it's not personal" line can seem a bit manipulative, whether intentional or not. If you push back on someone who says it with a "hey, man, that *IS* personal," the implication can be that you just aren't business-minded. Or worse, that you can't handle the pressures that come with the life of a pro — maybe your skin needs to be, you know, *thicker*.

It's a mean corner to back someone into because all they can do is to "feel" something (rarely joy) and try like heck to pretend they don't feel it at all.

How many times does someone say, "It's not personal; it's business, and by the way, you're doing a flippin' *fantastic* job. Here's a big ol' raise!"?

Know of any of these moments?

Me neither.

We might not like to admit it, especially when trying to be a "professional" — it's not even cool in some business circles to show your feelings (more on that later) — but feelings are exactly what we have throughout the day. And so do your employees.

Tired of that word yet? I hope not. I'm going to say it a lot. So bear with me; there's a method to my madness — or a *purpose*, you might say.

I'll be saying that word a lot too.

SO WHY SAY IT?

We often say, "It's not personal," to let ourselves off the hook. It's similar to its distant cousin, "It's not you, it's me." Both deliver an ouch, and both are used to get us out of the hot seat.

But in reality, they only make the other person feel more *personally* about things than ever, and we are in fact sitting in the very hot seat that delivered it.

There are times when business decisions are necessary based on finances, markets, economic downturns, etc. But it's still personal to the employee being affected; telling them it's not is like trying to make them feel bad for feeling bad.

HUMANS NEED PURPOSE

Even though artificial intelligence's abilities are growing in leaps and bounds, your employees are all still probably human — with emotions. In fact, the same ones we've always had. We haven't invented any new ones that I'm aware of. Whether you believe that we were created or that we evolved, or that the big bang theory explains it all, the truth is that we all *are* human. And we are all emotional.

Somewhere along the line, we were told not to show our feelings to maintain a certain professional "presence." What kind of presence *is* that, exactly? If you're human, you can't *help* but have emotions. Is it true that the more you pretend you're *not* having them, the more professional you are?

I don't buy it.

Seems silly to not let on that you're feeling something. There are limits, of course. You can't throw your feelings around just because you want to or because you lack self-control. That's no good either.

We'll come back to that later.

But getting too caught up in presence can come across as fake to your team. Worse, it also suggests that leaders should be fake. And teams don't like fake anything.

Do you?

Your Customers Are Probably Human Too

As far as I know, your customers are people too. The decision-makers, the leaders, the owners, the end users, and so on... all humans, right?

Of course, there are systems now that automate parts of the process from counting to ordering to delivering in some cases. But the ones buying those cornflakes from you are not robots. And your employees are typically the ones interacting with those buyers on the front line.

Ever been to a place where the person waiting on you was clearly not into what they were doing? Yep, me too.

How about a place where the employee was clearly just the opposite — energetic, attentive, and seemed to take pride in serving you? Also, yep. Those are the places we go back to and tell our BFFs about.

That's because we *enjoy* them more, and we feel taken *care* of on some level. We *like* it there, and we probably go back again and again to places like that.

Great service says, "Thank you, please come back." Poor service says, "Come back or don't; up to you." Which treatment would bring you back again and again?

Exactly.

Bottom line: Great service never, as in never *ever*, goes out of style. People who are happy at their jobs just naturally provide better customer service to the customers they interact with.

Consider how your people appear to customers and the outside world. Does their behavior reflect something you're teaching by how you're leading your team — even by accident?

Creating Purpose

Purpose.

There's that other word I'll be sharing a lot — and it's a big one. It's also personal, and we're all seeking it.

Your teams want to feel a sense of purpose in what they do at work. Don't we all?

Purpose is what drives us and encourages us to push forward. It makes us feel a part of something bigger, less alone. It helps us feel that what we're doing and contributing is valued and important.

Because it is.

Purpose wasn't just created with Generation A, B, or C, or X, Y, or Z. Purpose is seriously old-school, but it's *never* gone out of style (and never will). The difference is that current generations are speaking up about the importance of it. I, for one, applaud that.

Unlike past generations who moved the widgets all day but had to wait until they punched out to find joy, employees today are saying, "Nah, man... I want to know what my purpose is right *here* at work right now." That's because teams *want* to work with their hearts, understanding the why of the organization and how they contribute to it.

So how do we make that happen for them? How do we create workplaces of joy and purpose for our teams, while growing the business?

Read on, fair leader... read on.

> **Purpose is seriously old-school, but it's *never* gone out of style (and never will).**

Your Company Has a Purpose Too

Every company has a purpose.

The focus of yours might be to make those cornflakes we mentioned earlier, or to make the bowls they are poured into at breakfast.

Whether you're a bowl maker or a cornflake producer, the real purpose in all of that is to feed people in some way. Every function, person, and process comes down to getting those flakes to someone who needs or wants them.

Thinking of it that way changes how your team sees their role in your organization — how they're serving others. That's an important shift and it's one that speaks to the heart of what teams want.

Service. It's purposeful, and it's personal. And it's a powerful driver for you and your team to be clear on and come into work each day with.

Purpose and the Bottom Line

You may be wondering whether all this purpose stuff "brings home the bacon," so to speak, and impacts the bottom line.

The numbers are indeed affected by a great workplace and culture. Data indicates that one of the main things defining a great workplace for today's talent is a sense of purpose.

First, bringing purpose into the workplace is the right thing to do. Second, believe it or not, while "purpose" may not be a line item on your financials or on any spreadsheet, it's in there.

Last, the bonus is that leading from a place of purpose creates more energy in your organization and team than you can imagine. A total win-win.

The Numbers Tell the Story

Numbers matter to all leaders because if the business isn't making money, *no one* in it is thriving.

But while the numbers may not tell the whole story, they *do* tell how *well* the story is going. The following information speaks to companies considered to have a great culture and may be the proof that purpose really *is* in the financials.

What the Employees of the Best Places Have to Say

In 2018, Great Place to Work® published an analysis based on *Fortune* magazine's 100 Best Companies to Work For®,[4] based solely on the anonymous votes of employees.

The report included what they felt would be the key trends for workplace culture based on their research:

1. A fairer workplace
2. Increased focus on development
3. A deeper sense of purpose

Not a lot in there about pay and benefits, although those things are important. However, what this says is that what talent today is seeking, even demanding, in the workplace are some very personal things.

Great Place to Work® also compared the financial results for the publicly traded Fortune 100 Best Companies to Work For® winners to the nonwinners. The results from the 2018 report showed that the Best Companies to Work For®

outperformed the nonwinners in the index with a return of about 2.5 times.

Not a small number.

Of course, a lot has happened since 2018, what with political turmoil and a little thing called COVID-19. So, you might be wondering whether this trend held.

It sure did.

Look at the chart shown in Figure 1.1, which shows cumulative results from 1998 to 2023.[5] Not only did the trend hold, but it *increased*. The Fortune 100 Best Companies to Work For® market return average increased to *almost four times* that of the nonwinners.

Figure 1.1

Stock Comparison of Average vs. 100 Best Companies

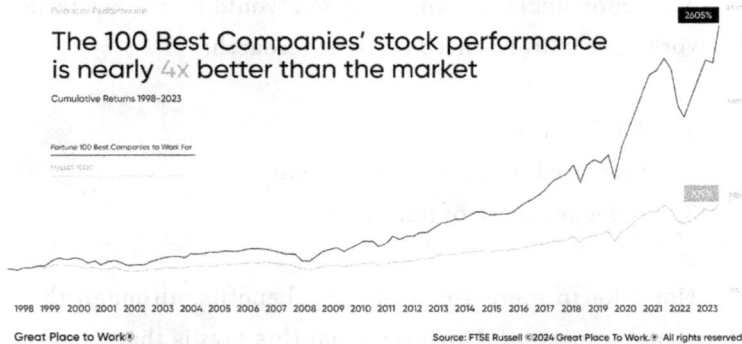

The 100 Best Companies' stock performance is nearly 4x better than the market

Cumulative Returns 1998-2023

Fortune 100 Best Companies to Work For

Russell 1000

2605%

705%

1998 1999 2000 2001 2002 2003 2004 2005 2006 2007 2008 2009 2010 2011 2012 2013 2014 2015 2016 2017 2018 2019 2020 2021 2022 2023

Great Place to Work®   Source: FTSE Russell ©2024 Great Place To Work.® All rights reserved.

(Source: Great Place to Work® used by permission)

But wait — there's more.

Seems the best companies in the survey had another feather in their caps: They experienced an average of one-half of the turnover of the other companies.[6]

With turnover costing businesses an average of six to nine months of salary to replace an employee,[7] that's not a tiny number.

The moral of this story? Happy employees produce more, stick around longer, and make for a happier bottom line, which is far more likely when the organizational culture is a good one.

That should make the hearts of you number lovers go pitter-patter.

Mine sure did.

CULTURE IS MADE OF PEOPLE

Nowadays, a great culture is something people are paying attention to, and more successful leaders aren't afraid to say their *people* are number one. That's often an example of a great culture.

That great talent you're looking for is seeking companies with cultures focused on their development. Great talent (*and great leadership*), after all, drives growth.

Because culture is personal.

In fact, organizational culture is defined as the "personality" of a company[8] and includes management style, employee behaviors, ethics, values, and more — none of which is calculated by an Excel formula.

I prefer my own, shorter definition of a company's culture: It is how the people there treat each other. That sums it up nicely.

If the people treat each other well, you can bet that culture nurtures that behavior and requires the people who work there to have it.

ARE YOU GUILTY OF USING
ANY OF THESE "HALL PASSES"?

Like the phrase "It's not personal," there are other disclaimers — I like to call them "hall passes" — people sometimes use to get through delivering bad news. Whether intentional or not, they instantly set up a negative vibe that can put the receiver on edge.

"May I be brutally honest?" *Must* you be brutal? If what you're about to say is honest and true, just say it. Drop the brutal.

"Let me be blunt." No need to be blunt; just be honest. Being truthful comes from the heart, making it easier to hear and process.

"I'm just direct." Alrighty, so be direct. But don't set people up by letting honesty with an edge take the rap for delivering news a little more sharply than necessary. Just tell them the truth, simply and calmy.

"Constructive criticism." We *ALL* know that when someone says this, they're about to lay some serious red ink on something you did or said. Keep it simple; just call it feedback. That's what it is, right?

"I just tell it like it is." This is adding energy and electricity to something that doesn't need it. Just be honest; leave out the jolt.

WHAT TO DO INSTEAD

Hopefully you're with me now on the personal nature of work, and in realizing that companies with great cultures outperform companies without them.

What else should you consider?

First Off, Don't Say It

It's best to just say that you know how the situation you're telling them about is going to affect them.

Give them the truth. If it's about a decision that had to be made for economic reasons, say that.

Then take a moment to understand, and even observe, what they're feeling. Give them a moment to process how they're feeling, if possible.

Accept the Emotions

Remain cool, calm, and collected, even in a storm. Find a way to accept the emotions, yours and your team's, that come with the day-to-day — including challenging situations.

Learn to process your own emotions but not be ruled by them. This skill will add value to any message you may need to deliver or receive.

The bonus here is that emotions create a fantastic teaching moment. Modeling calm in sticky situations is a great example for those new leaders you're developing. They'll undoubtedly pay that skill, and value, forward with their own teams.

One More Thing

I read an article on the origins of the phrase "It's not personal; it's just business." Turns out it was not birthed from the movie *The Godfather*, as many believe.

Actually, according to the article, this phrase is attributed to one Otto Berman, an accountant for organized crime families.[9]

I'll just leave that there.

CHAPTER TWO

#2

THERE ARE NO BRILLIANT JERKS ON A DREAM TEAM

Know any super-duper dream teams in the workplace that have a bunch of jerks on them? Even super-duper-smart jerks? Probably not. And your team would agree. Jerks aren't popular, and they are zero fun to work with (or for).

Don't get me wrong, I love smart people. But some of the smartest among us aren't so bright when it comes to knowing how they impact others, especially if they are in a leadership position.

So let me start with this: *Intelligence is not a weapon.*

Intelligence is best used in service to others, to get things done that promote that mission. It's not a tool for manipulation. I'll say that another way for the back row: If you use intelligence

23

as a weapon, you're a jerk, and jerks make terrible leaders.

I've witnessed times when someone is downright brilliant but is quick to let others know they are. I'll even bet there was a person or two who came to mind the minute you read those last

> Intelligence is best used in service to others, to get things done that promote that mission. It's not a tool for manipulation.

few sentences. I know I've experienced a few people in my life who were very smart but let others know it by their expression, impatience, tone, actions, direction (or lack of), exclusion, or just plain old-fashioned disregard.

When you think about it, though, attempting to impress someone with your brilliance is pretty dumb. If you're a leader, your whole goal is to motivate your team to grow and be successful. Trying to make someone feel "less than" will *not*, I repeat, *not* motivate them at all.

Why on earth would a team stick around to be treated this way?

They won't.

Further, while they are being subjected to this type of behavior, they won't be engaged, excited about the job before them, interested in the company's success, or learning anything from you.

SO, WHAT DO I MEAN BY A JERK?

Often, when I ask this while speaking or facilitating a leadership development program, I get suggestions about jerkesque behaviors that include:

- Rudeness
- Dishonesty
- Taking credit for others' work
- Bullying
- Playing favorites
- Unfriendliness
- Lack of caring
- Unfairness
- Unkindness
- Argumentativeness
- Unapproachability
- Not listening
- Egotism

Feel free to add any that I missed.

Whenever I'm speaking on the subject and ask the audience about this, it's as if a situation they experienced in the past just happened five minutes ago. To them, and to your team, it can feel like that, even after many years.

How you treat people is *that* powerful, and it carries an even greater weight with your team because you are their leader.

I think of all those things and more when I reflect on jerks I've known in my past.

Here's the kicker: When you're thinking about those jerks, turn that thought around and point it at yourself. Have *you* ever been any of those things?

I know I have, and I'm not proud of it. Not one bit. We all have, even when we didn't mean to. Probably even you.

The good news is that you can make up for it starting today, as in right now.

KEEPING DERRICK IN MIND

I remember a time in my career when my boss reprimanded me in front of a group of people, and it was ugly. The thing that had triggered her was silly, but she totally blew her top.

I was still pretty new in my career, and my nature was to try to work extra hard and give it all I had. So, I was extra devastated by her words and horribly embarrassed that she delivered them in front of several others. Just as bad, I could see that the others were embarrassed *for* me, including my own direct reports. They were just as horrified as I was at her outburst.

Somehow, shaking in my pumps, I summoned the courage to politely say I appreciated the feedback but felt it would be more appropriate to have a separate conversation to resolve the issue. She blew up even harder and louder, but only for a quick second this time, and I stood my ground.

Was I crazy? Yes, I was. But in that moment, I remembered Derrick's story and the impact that it had on him, *and* on me. Standing up for myself may have been a stupid thing for me to do, but honestly, it felt good even if I was seriously scared in that moment.

So, I suggested the private conversation and stood still. She simmered down and moved on with her discussion. Afterward, though, one of the witnesses to the storm thanked me for my show of respect — not for the boss, but for myself. I never got an apology from my boss for her outburst, but somehow my teammate's words of thanks mattered even more.

My boss never did anything like that again, at least not to me. Had I somehow set a boundary? Maybe. I'd like to think it was a moment in which I grew, and so did my boss.

Wow, I remember that like it was yesterday, too. It wasn't, though; it was a very long time ago. And, just like the harsh words she used that day, the fact that it changed our relationship somehow is a vivid memory too.

I never forgot that moment, and I never forgot that my boss was capable of humiliating me without a second thought. I may have gained some ground that day in my own sense of confidence, but our relationship lost something. It was never quite the same.

It's like that with your team too. Even though they may act like everything's okay the next day, it's not. They're holding onto that moment of being demeaned or witnessing it happening to a teammate, and they're likely looking for another workplace that won't allow that behavior. The memory is seared in their minds for a long time to come, and their energy now goes into avoiding that situation instead of making fabulous things happen at their job.

REMEMBER HOW IT FELT

Even if it's been a while since you were an up-and-comer, think back and remember how it felt when someone was a jerk to you. Please don't let time or status allow you to forget those moments — they are great lessons and guidance on being a better leader. You don't want to pay that feeling forward to anyone.

This isn't about not correcting folks when it's appropriate — mistakes and bad behaviors must be addressed at times. That's another important part of leadership and is also part of helping your team advance.

They get that and ultimately will understand that they grow from it.

What I'm referring to here, though, is the intention of just being a jerk, which means the intent is to hurt someone or wield some sort of power.

Teams don't like jerks, aren't inspired by them, and are not motivated to work harder from their hearts when led by one. They never forget being humiliated or belittled, and never ever forget that when you do make them feel that way, they can't fight back. Not really.

Correct them when you must, but always let your team keep their dignity. Also, keep your intention focused on helping them develop. Then they won't come away feeling beaten down and are likely to feel that you care enough to help them grow.

SO WHY DO WE ACT THIS WAY?

Why on earth do we as leaders sometimes act like jerks?

Most likely something else is going on that may be related to how we were led or taught early in our careers. Perhaps someone we looked up to early on acted badly and we're modeling them. We could have been taught that showing others how smart we are means acting like a jerk or that we are given a "pass" to act like that if we believe we're smarter.

It could also just be that we have adopted some bad habits and haven't yet developed the self-awareness to notice they are not working for us (more on this coming up).

Or it could even be that our own lack of confidence is driving us to behave in this way.

Could be *all* the above.

But whatever the reason, acting this way doesn't work when we're leading a team because it points the focus inward and not on the team. And it doesn't give the team what they need most — inspiration and focus on their growth.

BUILD YOUR EMOTIONAL INTELLIGENCE

The *smartest* among us might be brilliant as far as our IQ says, but our EQ (emotional intelligence quotient) score might be a different matter.

I guarantee you that a high-EQ person would not be considered a jerk by their team. They would have developed a good level of self-awareness and an awareness of their impact on the people around them (including their team).

Leaders should inspire and motivate their teams. After all, that's one of the main things teams want from their leaders. Remember, these days these teams are the folks who want to work with their hearts and a sense of purpose; inspiration and motivation kind of go along with that.

In addition, they want to grow and feel accomplished, and this, in turn, is what will grow your business. Unless you are planning on doing everything in your company yourself, you need some people with you. My guess is you also want them fully engaged and even on fire for what the company does and how it serves others.

But note that "engaged" and "on fire" in this context are... drumroll please... *feelings*.

Yessssssssss, we're back to that. Spell it with me: P-E-R-S-O-N-A-L.

Make Them the Center of Things

Getting a team engaged in what they do at work means making *them* the focus, and that starts with connecting to them, showing interest in who they are. It's more than just saying, "How was your weekend?" while you continue to walk briskly by on a Monday morning. That kind of "drive-by" greeting doesn't encourage engagement, and teams rightly take from this that you really aren't interested. They see you coming (and then keep on going), and it translates to them that you're just going through the motions of being friendly. If we're honest here (and we are), that's exactly what you're doing — just going through the motions.

Really connecting to your team is about taking time to talk with them, really getting to know what they want. You're doing that because you want to know, not because it's on your to-do list.

Ask them, with genuine interest, and then deeply listen to what they say. And don't stop there. Take any steps possible to help them make the things they want to happen come true.

You can do this by mentoring, helping them to open doors, and even teaching and coaching them. Nothing says "I believe in you" like investing in someone's growth. This is a subject I'm very passionate about; in fact, I have a whole Truth Bomb devoted to it later in this book. Stay tuned for that one.

The smartest and best leaders out there make their team feel like total rock stars. And if you've chosen your team well, that's exactly what they are. Let them know that by showing your interest in who they are. Learn about them and what they are dreaming for in their lives; and for goodness' sake, talk to them — while standing still.

Model Something Great

Think carefully about the kind of pay-it-forward examples leaders should be practicing. Are you modeling those?

Help your team become great leaders themselves by modeling something great. Just as they'll never forget a jerk, they'll also never forget a great leader who cared about them.

Given how hard it is to find and keep great talent, consider that the word will get out as to how people are treated at your organization. There is no shortage of websites devoted to letting people know about this or that company's leadership, and don't kid yourself — they're popular and widely used, most likely by former or even current employees. Don't be a subject on one of those sites for having bad behavior, and don't let other leaders in your organization end up there, either. Because, once that bell rings, it's out there ringing for a *very* long time.

It's better to create a culture where team members feel comfortable talking to you, not filling out a survey about you. Remember? It's personal. You can't build that kind of culture while also acting like a jerk... even if you don't mean to be. You can't have it both ways. Something's gotta give. And that's gotta be you. You're the leader. It's part of your responsibility. Speaking of which...

Let Them Be the Smart Ones

Here's an idea: Just start asking your team what they think.

I've been asked many times by leaders how they could figure out what their team was thinking and what they wanted. I'd always respond with, "Well, ask them."

Your team will tell you. They *want* to tell you, and when they do, it's hands down the best way to find out what's really going on with them, as well as how to lead them better by addressing those things.

Let them solve problems. If you don't like their solutions, let them come up with better ones. It's not about you being smart. It's about them learning.

Ask Them to Rate You

How do the team members think you're doing as a leader? Finding this out can be accomplished with a simple conversation, particularly if a culture of openness and feedback is present. A survey can also be used, providing anonymity to the employees responding, which is highly recommended. If you want their true opinion, give them safety to offer it.

A word of caution, though: Once you ask for their feedback, be prepared to hear it — and I mean *all* of it. Then also be prepared to respond with a simple "thank you."

Period. That's it. Just "thank you."

Take it all in, don't react, don't respond to anything in the survey — not yet anyway. Let it rest and ask yourself whether any of it, positive or negative, is true.

Here's another tip: If something really gets your goat in the feedback, it's probably true, at least in part. That one will probably sting a little, but trust me, you'll be the better for it if you read it and pause.

Surveys like this can be pure gold in terms of improving your leadership style and leading a team better. But it only works if you're willing to hear what they have to say and then show that you appreciate their candor by working to improve. That takes some humility, which is much better for leading your team than being a jerk.

There's a bonus to surveying your team — they learn that you care what they think. They may have wanted to share some things for a long time, and you've just given them the chance to, so buckle in. The flow will eventually slow a bit, but in the meantime you're about to hear it all.

And you should also be grateful for every bit of feedback. It will help you be a better leader.

You might just get some amazing information, and some great advice on what the team needs from you and your organization to reach their full potential. Who doesn't want that? Their full potential means the organization reaches its own full potential as well.

Remember, teams fully plugged in are creating organizations that grow and are electric with energy, the right kind.

Doesn't that sound fantastic?

Your team likes that idea a whole lot, and they want you to know what they believe will help you all get there together.

#3

YOU CAN'T CHERRY-PICK WHO TO BE KIND TO

You're either kind or you're not.

This might be my favorite "LTB." Wait, no. Wait — yes, it totally is. Well, maybe... No, definitely *yes...*

Oh, heck, they're all my faves.

But I have to say that this one always pings me down deep when I read it or say it in a workshop. I think that's because it sums up nicely that kindness is a way of being, and *not* a tool for rewarding only some people or behaviors.

Selective kindness doesn't sit well with anyone, mainly because it looks a lot like favoritism. And that's because it is.

THE DANGERS OF FAVORITISM

Oh dear. It's 2025 (at the time of writing) and we're *still* hearing about how negative favoritism is in the workplace. I haven't heard anyone yet proclaim the virtues of it, nor have I seen it used as a great benefit in any recruiting ads — "Come work with us! We're rife with favoritism! Yeehaw!"

I'm being silly here, but don't miss my point. Your team, *everyone's* team at any level in the organization, hates favoritism.

Here's why:

IT'S WRONG.

And that's just for starters.

Favoritism is often defined as rewarding people for a reason other than merit. In other words, rewarding someone because of who they are, or how you know them, versus a skill they possess or something they've done well. In the workplace, merit is an important distinction in this regard because, at the end of the day, employees are there to create or perform something they are tasked with doing. They should be rewarded because of their skill at doing that.

Hiring best friends, family, and so on — even when they have seriously mad skills and are total rock star producers — puts a big red "F" on their shirts. You can use a variety of endings to complete that word... but in this case it stands for "Favorite." Even if they're downright phenoms, they'll have to work harder than everyone else just to escape the assumption that they're doing well only *BECAUSE* they're your favorite.

It's often a no-win situation.

Favoritism is doubly tricky because even the perception of favoritism by your team is a problem. Perception, after all, is what many a judgment is made from.

Even Hobbies Can Be Danger Zones

Even though not necessarily illegal, showing what looks like favoritism simply because of a shared hobby or interest can sometimes get you into hot water. Even if the practice is not meant to exclude others, if a team member perceives they are not being noticed because they aren't part of a circle of friends or a group the boss is hanging with, they can feel resentment and isolation.

They may be focused on how to get on the good side of the higher-ups by adopting likes, dislikes, styles, habits, and who knows what else to be part of the cool gang that's getting all the attention.

Guess what that means?

Exactly: The energy is not on growing and productivity. And changing just to be accepted results in frustration and ultimately resentment for their leader AND the leader's circle of favorites.

Worse, the situation can demotivate the heck out of them in a flash if they feel like they can't get into the "inner circle."

These kinds of situations can happen by accident without anyone realizing they're creating that kind of feeling. But there's another way favoritism can happen, and it's even worse. So I'll say it now...

... KINDNESS IS NOT A STRATEGY

Let me say this loud and right up front: Kindness is *not* a handy-dandy trick to get people to work harder or do more. You can't fake it. Not even for a second.

> Kindness is *not* a handy-dandy trick to get people to work harder or do more.

Your team can sniff out a lack of genuine kindness in a jiffy. They may not understand fully what feels "off" about a "kindness faker," but they know something isn't sitting right, and they instinctively don't trust that person. Being a jerk is bad enough, but faking kindness can be even worse.

Just don't do it.

We admire kind people, look up to them, aspire to *be* them, yet we don't always recognize that they are actually the strongest and smartest among us. It feels different to engage with someone who is kind just for the sake of kindness and nothing more.

Truly kind folks don't ever use kindness to motivate people to do more of something or complete a project on time, or other such things. They're being kind just because they ARE kind. See the difference?

People respond to those genuinely kind souls and are naturally motivated by them because true kindness is encouraging. It sends a wonderful energy to people who receive it or witness it. There's a response inside that feels "right" about someone's genuine kindness, and the reaction is typically positive.

How do you feel after an act of giving? Chances are you feel pretty darn good, right? I highly doubt you're vowing to never do it again, because it does feel great to be of service to others.

I believe this is because we're divinely wired to be helpful and kind to each other, and so we react to it in a positive way. We may not always get this right, but ask yourself how you feel the next time you are kind to someone, and see what you come up with.

I'm betting it's good.

We see a lot of cutesy, greeting card–esque remarks about kindness being strong. Well, it's *TRUE*.

Imagine, if you will, that time someone was being a real jerk to you, and you were trying to stay cool, calm, and collected. Was that easy? Heck, no! Controlling your emotions takes strength of character, focus, and commitment. I'm not talking about suppressing emotions, but rather acknowledging them and choosing to see them, and yet not spew them.

It's not always easy to be kind. It's just always worth the effort. Kindness can take many forms, which can include things such as thoughtful gifts and favors, but I think the easiest and most effective is often the least expensive — like a simple "thank you." It's kind to acknowledge the goodness and thoughtfulness of others, and these two little words get the job done with big impact.

Manners are also a form of kindness, and they *never* go out of style. I have yet in my life to find a situation where someone preferred to be around people without them — manners, that is. I think they are a show of respect to others, and what could be more kind than showing respect?

My last, and perhaps favorite, way of showing kindness is by listening. I once heard Deepak Chopra, author and alternative medicine advocate, say something to the effect that the best way to show someone you love them is by listening fully to what they're saying. I think he's right too.

Kind people have bad days too, maybe even have a little temper flare now and then. They're human too, after all. But kind folks clean up their emotional mishaps and right any wrongs ASAP. And the beautiful thing about it is people can tell when a genuinely kind person is truly apologizing. The misstep is forgivable in most cases, because the intention is to be kind. People feel it.

Your team feels it too.

HOW TO SHOW KINDNESS FAIRLY

We all know *HOW* to be kind... don't we?

You'd think so, and yet it can be a little different in the workplace at times. There are manners, politeness, etc., all good parts of being kind. But in a situation of leadership, teams look for additional types of kindness, fairly given, from their leaders, and your team is no exception.

Be Self-Aware to Include Everyone

Okay, I know I've already shown you why you shouldn't allow favoritism to creep in, even when you don't mean to. But how the heck do you keep from doing something you might not even realize you're doing?

Awareness.

It's human nature to be drawn to those we just instinctively know or feel commonality with. We can't always help it, but as a leader, you're just going to have to try.

Become and remain aware of your tendencies to naturally want to spend more time with certain people for whatever reason. Don't avoid those people, mind you, but just intentionally remember to include *all* of your team as equally as you can. It's fine to connect with those who have a hobby similar to yours, but it's just as important to intentionally connect with those who have a hobby you're not into. So, even if basket weaving isn't your thing, if it's a thing for someone on your team, ask them about it now and then.

I'll challenge you to even take it further. Intentionally add diversity to your team and be aware of how it takes things up a notch. Diversity broadens a team's perspective and brings in yummy, fresh new ideas. You want those, right? And the cool thing is team members are dying to tell you their ideas. They really are. They just want a safe place to do it. Give them one, and you'll *never* regret it.

Lastly on this point, taking favoritism out of the mix models and teaches fairness in a way that is hard to top. Your team is watching you, how you handle things, how you treat everyone, and how you treat them. Being fair and not practicing favoritism will tell them more than any workshop ever will. It builds safety and trust, and teams long for both.

You see, your team is using your behavior as a way to figure out what you and your organization want from them. They want to use that information to advance in the organization. Make sure you're showing them what you want that to be.

Show Equal Time

Take care to connect with your team as equally as you can. This can be tricky. After all, some need more from you than others.

But still, being available to them equally in proportion to how much they need you is a great place to start. So, here, just notice who needs you and when. And be careful not to assume only the loudest and most talkative ones are the ones who need you. The quiet ones need you too; they just may not be comfortable saying it out loud.

This reminds me of a situation I had years ago. There was an employee who told another leader that I didn't like them very much.

I was shocked. I actually thought very highly of this employee and felt she was smart as a whip. She was quiet and introverted but a real rock star when it came to getting things done and done right. I thought she was downright fabulous. She still is.

So where did the disconnect come from?

I had a morning ritual of sauntering through the office floors and saying hello to various team members, stopping and chatting them up a bit to see how they were. Each morning, she was typically facing her computer working and didn't look up or acknowledge me as I walked by. I figured she was busy and didn't want to be interrupted, so, out of respect, I didn't speak to her and just kept going.

Turns out, she felt slighted when I didn't stop. Because I wasn't stopping, she assumed I didn't like her. It was an easy fix, and I immediately went to her, apologized, and vowed to never let it happen again. But I also asked that she give me some kind of cue that it was okay to stop and chat. Problem solved and a great working relationship ensued; and the morning hellos became even better.

I'll always be grateful to her for the lesson and for the honor of getting to know her a bit more and watch her grow. She's not only a rock star, but also a teacher who taught me something valuable that I'll never forget.

Accept People for Who They Are

There's a lot out there about DEI (diversity, equity, and inclusion) initiatives and their value. But I think it all really boils down to one thing to always remember: acceptance. We need to accept people right where they are and for who they are.

Is it really that simple?

Yep. It's really that simple.

What choice do you have, after all? *Not* accept them? I guess you could, but there they are. Still themselves.

Go with it and see what you can learn and give to all your team, as I said, right where they are. Pay attention to them as equally as you can, even the ones who don't turn around when you walk by. You may just find that your own skills as a leader level up big-time and you grow from it all.

You won't regret it.

And they won't forget it.

Practice Good Favoritism

I know.

I just spent all this time going on and on (and on) about how awful favoritism in the workplace is, saying that it's a bad "F" word, and how much your team wants you to know they would hate it if you did it. And now, here I go telling you when it works, right?

Well, it's a point I need to make.

Favoritism only works when you make *everyone* on your team your favorite.

See what I did there?

But it's true.

Make them *all* your favorites and make sure they know it too. How do you do this? Easy-peasy. Give them attention, time, focus. Make sure they know you value them and their indi-

> **Favoritism only works when you make *everyone* on your team your favorite.**

vidual personalities and contributions. Guide them, encourage them, course correct them when needed. But above all, be curious about what they want — their dreams and aspirations. Ask them questions about these things, and then help them get there.

This is a beautiful part of leadership and one of the most important things teams want from us — to help *them* grow and develop.

And as they grow, you will too.

CHAPTER FOUR

DON'T LOSE YOUR SH*T

Nobody else wants it.

No, really, they don't.

I get it. We're all human, and we all have our feelings, including anger. I've spent some time in this book explaining feelings and emotions and how important they are in leadership; but I'm going to shift gears a little and suggest that there may be times when you need to keep that emotional flood under control (and to yourself).

Your team absolutely, 100 percent does *not* like it when you lose your sh*t. As in, your temper.

Actually, *nobody* likes it. Anyone ever ask you to lose it because they love it so much? Exactly.

By the way, you look funny
to your team when you do lose it.

By the way, you look
funny to your team
when you do lose it.

TENNIS, ANYONE?

When I think about losing sh*t, I'm instantly reminded of
watching John McEnroe play tennis years ago. He wasn't a
leader of a big team in a big (or small) company that I'm aware
of, but he was a leader in his sport, and to me his story is very
relevant to the problems of losing your stuff.

Quick — what do you think of when I mention John
McEnroe? Fabulous tennis player? How many championships
he won? His biggest strength at the game? Probably not.

McEnroe was a well-known tennis professional in the
1980s and 1990s. He wouldn't have been on the television playing tennis at all the big matches if he had been a not-so-good
tennis pro, after all.

The problem is, no one remembers that McEnroe was a pretty great tennis player because his famous temper and outbursts
took all the attention away from his talent. I imagine that, even
generations since, those who weren't around to see his famous
meltdowns have heard about his nasty displays of temper.

It's a shame too. His skills were what brought him to the
limelight, but it was hard to notice them when you knew that
the emotional fireworks would start at any moment. To be honest, I think a lot of people tuned in just to wait and watch *that*
show instead of the tennis match at hand. I know I did.

Was this show of emotion a public relations stunt? Could
be. But it sure felt and looked like just a big ol' tantrum.

His famous lack of control cost him a lot too. Money, for one thing — I've read he received numerous fines and suspensions, and at times he lost prize money after screaming and swearing at officials and umpires. Even spectators weren't spared his fury.

I've also read that his relationships outside of the tennis courts suffered as his famous temper reportedly led to tensions with teams and other professionals.

What might he have accomplished if he had directed all that negative energy toward the game instead?

Might he have won more? Maybe. We'll never know for sure.

What we do know, however, is that he is remembered, even after all these years, for acting out on the court and losing his sh*t on a regular basis. Not nearly the same legacy as being a great tennis player, which I suspect he was.

Bummer, John. I was pulling for you.

LOSING YOUR SH*T TAKES A TOLL ON OTHERS

You'll get lots of attention when you lose your poop, but it may not be the kind you want (or the lasting picture you want in the minds of everyone who witnessed it). Teams are not wildly motivated by the spewing of anger or raised voices. They may perform better in response to it in that moment, but, trust me, their minds are still on your meltdown and how to avoid another one. And that worry hangs around for a long time.

Once a leader starts a tantrum (which is how a team views it), all of their energy, every speck of it, goes toward the flare-up. That's right — everyone in the vicinity has just directed all their energy to the show. They are no longer focused on the problem, project, or deliverable at hand.

Afterward, the tantrum still sucks up energy because people are completely focused on staying out of your crosshairs for the near future, and maybe longer. There is now a little voice in the back of their mind reminding them that you're capable of blowing a gasket. With that, the psychological *tiptoeing* begins. This is energy redirected toward self-preservation rather than productivity and creating cool new stuff.

Companies don't take leaps in innovation if their employees are walking on their psychological tippy toes. Tippy-toe walking can be stifling and even restrictive. Companies want and need big ideas, "wild thinking," I like to call it, to stay current, vibrant, and ahead of the competition.

Having teams who are afraid to share their yummy, fresh new ideas is not good for business. Are you one of those leaders who stifle creativity and safety in this way? If so, it's time for something different.

> **Companies don't take leaps in innovation if their employees are walking on their psychological tippy toes.**

WHAT'S THE UPSIDE OF LOSING YOUR SH*T?

There isn't one.

Bet you knew I was going to say that though.

Calm and collected is the best way to handle things... find that zone and stay there whenever possible.

You'll thank me later for this, and guess who else will? Your team.

Bet you knew I was going to say that too. But if you don't believe me, here are some experts who feel the same as I do.

STUDIES SHOW SELF-CONTROL IS BETTER

Let's go back to the topic of emotional intelligence and learn why it's important in these situations.

According to Socialigence, Michael Beldoch, a clinical professor of psychology at Cornell University, first coined the term "emotional intelligence."[10] But it was further popularized by Daniel Goleman in his 1995 book, *Emotional Intelligence: Why It Can Matter More Than IQ*. Goleman's book brought the subject back into the limelight and sparked many to think about its application in leadership.[11]

In a nutshell, our emotional intelligence quotient ("EQ") is about how we handle ourselves emotionally and how aware we are of the ways in which our emotions affect others. While important for everyone, it's downright *essential* for leaders to be keenly aware of the impact what they say and do has on others — remember Derrick.

This level of awareness begins, however, with understanding how your emotions are affecting *you*.

People who have developed a high EQ know what rattles them, what gets under their skin, and how they react to it. They have learned how to pay attention to their emotions and understand how others react to them. This increased self-awareness helps them understand the importance of controlling their tempers so that the conversation or situation is focused on the issue at hand, not their reaction.

This ability to regulate emotions and reactions supports open communication between leaders and their teams. Leaders with high EQ listen deeply to their teams. These leaders are easy to talk with, are approachable, and make careful, informed decisions. Because of these qualities, high-EQ leaders typically have earned the complete trust of their teams. It's easy to see why.

I believe the bottom line to EQ is what this chapter is all about — don't lose your sh*t. Guess what? If you keep your cool, you lose nothing, but you gain respect because your team will likely perceive you as someone who stays focused and uses all their energy to figure out the right, best move to make in a situation.

Yes, Daniel and I say it differently. He might just be nicer than I am. Probably is. I'm okay with that, though. I think Dan and I are on the same page here.

And I'm pretty sure he won't mind my calling him Dan.

THE LAST WORD ON SH*T (LOSING IT, THAT IS)

Sometimes someone acts unkindly, or is a jerk as discussed earlier, to let off steam. That someone might even be you.

But for leaders, letting off steam in the workplace is selfish. There's just no place for it in leadership. I'm hard-pressed to find the situation, even if the blast was justified, where it ended with great results. From the viewpoint of your team, or anyone else's nearby, it just looks like you don't have control of yourself. And if you can't control yourself, why should they trust you?

I understand all too well the pressures that come with leadership. They're not small. But I also understand that your team rarely knows all that you are dealing with.

News flash: It's not their job to know. That's *your* job.

They aren't the leader. They're there to perform their jobs and to be developed to support their growth and the growth of the company. It's your job as their leader to handle issues and challenges. Remember, your skill set is likely different from your team's or further developed than theirs is currently. You can't expect them to communicate and operate at a skill level they haven't grown to yet.

Because of that, it's nearly impossible for your team to be understanding about a tantrum. To them, one minute it's just business, the next minute it's a volcano eruption that makes no sense. This behavior seems erratic, and even silly. It definitely doesn't illustrate the leadership qualities they want to aspire to.

If you're not prepared to handle the stress of leadership without blowing your top, you may need to rethink things a bit. If you're someone who routinely flies off the handle in your personal life, consider that that's a habit you've formed and been allowed to continue. It's also a bad habit — and one your team doesn't need to see, nor do they care to.

It's also rarely aligned with the corporate culture that business leaders are trying (or should be trying) to build — a culture that encourages and nurtures their teams to their greatest potential.

Mistakes happen. Problems occur. Team members goof up or behave badly. Handling those things does not have to include a blowup. Read that again — blowing up is not required to handle an issue.

Tips for Keeping Your Cool

What to do when the poopie hits the fan, or you feel like you want to throw some around? Here are a few ideas you might want to try on for size:

- **Find another way** to handle conflicts without including everyone in the vicinity. Take the discussion behind closed doors, for instance.

- **Feel what you need to feel, but don't let anger or stress run you.** You're human, remember. You're allowed to be upset. Just consider your team. While they may care about you, they *don't* care to have you take emotions out on them, which is how it can feel to them.

- **Have cool-down mechanisms** you can practice out of eyesight and earshot of your team while you work through things. Walk away, shut your door, and breathe — and maybe even find that trusted leadership-level person to vent with and get their insight while you catch your breath and let the angry dust settle.

- **Remind yourself of the cost.** If you're prone to having a temper that goes from 0 to 60 in a nanosecond, you probably know that. Acknowledge it, and then also remember how long it took everyone to be comfortable around you again after the last time you lost your temper. Is losing it again worth the negative result?

Your team wants you to know they watch how you handle things and they're learning about you — what sets you off and what doesn't — as a result. That's time spent focusing on something other than what they're there for — is that energy wasted? Could be.

But they're also learning through your example how to handle stress and challenges as a leader. Ask yourself, "What am I teaching them?" when you go ballistic. Is that the trait you want them to become known for later in their career as well? Probably not.

In addition to keeping your heart rate at bay, as I've mentioned before, keeping your cool in the face of even the toughest of problems will garner great respect from your team and just about everyone else.

Remember, the gossip train is running, but it will carry the good stuff around too. Choo-chooooo.

CHAPTER FIVE

BEWARE OF FIFB

Oh dear.

The ol' FIFB, also known as first in, first believed.

Know those people who are the first ones to bolt like the wind into the boss's office with the latest juicy 411?

Know those bosses who tend to listen to, or worse *act* on, that information without doing any more checking?

Yeah, those are the ones I'm referring to. And I just bet someone came to mind when you read that just now. I've known a few of both, and man, is it ever a *dangerous* thing to do.

Now, I'm not referring to the people coming in to let the boss know something is happening that legitimately needs to be reported. Those things happen at times, and leaders are thankful for the info so they can address what needs to be addressed. In fact, it can be important to have a place where teams feel safe to do that.

In this chapter, however, I'm referring to people who can't wait to give *their* view on something to the corner office, with the sole intention of gossiping about it, or even skewing the story in the direction they'd like it to go. I'm also referring to leaders who can't seem to tell the difference between good and not-so-good intentions in this regard.

There's a difference, as I'm sure you know. I'm also sure your team knows it.

Practicing FIFB means you're reacting to the viewpoint of a single person — the first one to report the details. The problem is that the person is giving you *their* version. And they just may have it wrong.

> **Practicing FIFB means you're reacting to the viewpoint of a single person — the first one to report the details.**

Boy howdy, do teams notice this type of thing, and they don't like it — not one tiny bit.

I have my sister to thank for the inspiration behind this Leadership Truth Bomb.

Years ago, she told me of a situation at a place where she was working. The manager of her department there always acted on news she received from the *first* person who told her.

One day, an irate customer called the department manager, upset, and loudly complained about one of my sister's teammates. The customer claimed he had not been given proper notice about something.

The manager, instantly outraged by what the customer said, immediately took his side. After ending the call, the manager made a snappy beeline to the employee's desk. In front of others, including my sister, she accused the employee of not doing her job, not being thorough, and other things. It seemed as though she was preparing to fire the employee on the spot.

The teammate, keeping her cool but understandably upset, calmly pulled the customer's file and produced a copy of the notice letter to the manager. It *had* been sent to the customer, as required, and all in a timely fashion.

The customer was wrong. *Completely* wrong.

The manager, realizing what she'd done, apologized and went back and called the customer, explaining that the company had, in fact, delivered proper notice, which made everything all better for everyone. Right?

Nope.

The customer simmered down pretty quickly, but the manager's actions affected the employee, my sister, and anyone else who may have overheard the conversation. If it had been an isolated incident, the manager's apology might have sufficed, but it wasn't. She did it often — my sister just hadn't seen it yet. That manager had lost her team's trust. They all knew that she would believe what someone said about them without checking to verify whether it was true. Worse, she'd act on it, up to and including threatening their jobs — and she never seemed to learn. My sister learned all of this from talking to the others, but this was her first time seeing it happen in person.

From that moment on, my sister took great strides to carefully document everything she did, said, or took care of. This included conversations with the team, the manager, and *definitely* every single customer she worked with. She felt she always had to be ready to prove herself with evidence of having done her job should the day come when she was falsely accused, just as it had for her teammate. And I'll just bet she wasn't the only one who felt that way.

This was decades ago, and yet my sister was able to recount the story like it happened last Tuesday. She needed her job, as they all did, and now she felt that her manager might fire her simply because of what someone else said — whether it was true or not.

They all had to look over their shoulders every day because their manager gave herself permission to react, or better yet, act out, without giving them enough benefit of the doubt to at least fact-check what was brought to her. They had no choice.

I have to wonder about the extra time that team felt they had to take to constantly be on guard. The stress of it all. Can you imagine? Not to mention the hits their morale and their sense of being valued must have taken.

Not only does FIFB mean you're getting only one side of the story, but it also means there is a high probability that this side is coming from a favorite of yours (or someone who *wants* to be). At the very least, it's someone who feels comfortable enough to dash in and give you the details because you've listened to them before. Just as bad, it's usually someone paying a whole lot of attention to what's going on versus what they *should* be doing — work.

Sounds like gossip to me.

Well, that's because it probably is.

And that's what your team thinks of it too. Even if they're gossiping about it themselves, they expect you *not* to. You're the leader after all, right? Like it or not, when you buy into that first story you hear, that's what they think you're doing.

Open the front door, because trust just left the building — again.

THE PROBLEMS WITH FIFB

One of the problems with FIFB is that the "informant" delivering the latest and greatest to you is going to be labeled exactly that and will likely be outcast by the rest of your team. If the person is one of your faves, that just makes them stick to you even more, and, you guessed it: The more they do, the more outcast they'll be by the others.

Oh, the team will tolerate them and may even pretend to be friendly — after all, they're trying to not be the latest headline on the office newswire — but they've likely already decided that person is *not* to be trusted. Unfortunately, the leader becomes part of the "don't trust" group as well.

The biggest problem with FIFB, though, is that you just don't have the whole story. Period. You have only one person's report. People are human, and they tend to be emotional about office problems as well. It's also human nature to focus on the points of the story that validate what the person may have already believed about the issue or person involved.

> You just don't have the whole story. Period. You have only one person's report.

Early in my career, one of my team members — we'll call her Debbie — went above me to my boss, who I'll call Jennifer, and complained that I was "tough" (not "too tough," mind you, just "tough"). She insinuated that I was treating her unfairly. Jennifer, legitimately wanting to hear Debbie out, listened to her complaint.

Unfortunately, Jennifer all but bought Debbie's story without much more information and subsequently spoke to me with the attitude that I needed to be corrected in some way.

To be fair, Jennifer's actions of taking in the complaint and then following up on it with me were 100 percent the right thing to do. I appreciated her openness to chat with an employee and the willingness to solve the problem. It was admirable.

However, Debbie had only given Jennifer *part* of the story.

Debbie hadn't mentioned that she had been misbehaving and causing massive disruption — not just on her own team, but on other teams too. In addition to gossiping about others, Debbie was blatantly handling one of her important tasks in a way I had expressly told her not to months prior, when I first caught her doing it. When I discovered the mishandling the second time, I verbally reprimanded her.

As I explained all of this to Jennifer, I was calm, clear, and to the point. There was no sugarcoating the fact that though Debbie had already been warned, she had decided to keep doing things her way. I therefore had to reprimand her again, warning her that a third violation would result in termination.

Once I explained this to Jennifer, she understood much better and told me I had taken the correct actions.

This situation is such a great example of how FIFB can result in problems.

First, you just don't know the whole story until you ask the right people for their version. Debbie was not about to share things such as her blatant insubordination with Jennifer. Her focus was on making me the bad guy (or gal, in this case) and skewing the conversation in that direction.

Second, it's a good way to damage relationships with your subordinates. Yes, Jennifer did come to me, which I appreciated, but almost with the assumption I was in the wrong. Had she reserved judgment until she got all the facts from Debbie, her discussion with me would have been quite different; I'm certain of that.

Though it ended all right and backfired on Debbie in the end, I still had to defend myself against judgment I didn't deserve. It shows how quickly *not* getting the full story can spiral out of hand and create way more drama, and waste of time and effort, than should ever be necessary.

That's what makes it even more important to not take a story hook, line, and sinker. The employee may not even mean to, but in these situations, they often try to skew your opinion to theirs. It's rare, if ever, for the person to run and say, "OMG, did you hear??? I only know a little part of the story, but I can't stand Johnny Doe anyway, so let me tell you what I believe he did to screw up!"

My guess is that hasn't happened. But objectivity is a perspective your team wants you to hang on to. You can only do that by being aware of who's typically running in to share the details, what you've observed about them before, and what you really know about the issue.

If you don't know much about a situation, do some asking around if you feel it's important enough.

THE ABCS OF AVOIDING FIFB

That's a lot of letters, but taking this subject down to basics is important. It's one I want to help you understand well so that you can get clarity on how your team sees it and feels about it.

Welcome Information from Everyone

It's important that your office door is open equally for all, and not just the one or two folks who can't wait to gain your favor with their version of the latest and greatest. They may not even be aware that's what they're doing, but that's how it looks to the rest of the team (who don't trust them).

Intentionally encourage others to share with you — seek out new opinions. You might try reiterating that anyone is welcome to talk to you when the chance arises. Remind them in team meetings and gatherings.

Encourage the Right Intentions

You don't want people to feel they shouldn't tell you a thing, but you want people to develop a sense of what their intention is behind it. And that intention should be to solve a situation or conflict and make something better in some way.

Coach them on how to identify what their intention is by asking themselves that question. Make it a part of their development. One day when they're leaders, their own teams will be grateful.

Be Slow to Act and React

Don't forget Leadership Truth Bomb #4 (you know, the one about not losing your sh*t). You don't want to look funny forever in the minds of your team. Reactions can cause more reactions if you don't slow things down.

At first, just hear the words the team member is saying; don't internalize them just yet. You don't know the other side. Take a moment to think it through, and don't do *anything* right off the bat. Nothing.

> **Take a moment to think it through, and don't do *anything* right off the bat.**

Intentionally pause to reflect for a moment and make sure you aren't having any knee-jerk judgments or reactions to what you've been told.

And then, let it breathe just a little. Give your reactions a moment to process, and another moment for your smarts to kick in and ask, "What's the best thing I can do for my team next?"

Monitor what's going on with you and notice if something else has your pulse higher than normal. If you can, put the issue aside for a bit. You can come back to it later — chances are it's not going anywhere.

Get All the Information Before Acting

No matter what the person is telling you about, vow to get all the information before taking any action.

This includes considering who's doing the reporting.

Notice who dashes in more regularly than others, and notice your reaction to what they're saying.

For instance, if the reporter of the crime is a close friend, you've doubtless spent time over cocktails discussing things in life that you both feel strongly about. But this is not buddy time. This is leader time. Find a way to avoid the cocktail-hour vibe when dealing with office issues.

When you have the person's story, seek the viewpoint of others.

A word of caution here, though: Make sure you're not seeking the same folks every time, or the ones who might have a biased perspective. That includes being aware of cliques or groups that might have an interest in taking a side.

It is a bit of human nature to form groups such as cliques, but it's your job as a leader to be aware of and avoid falling, or even *appearing* to fall, victim to their activities.

In fact, the subject of cliques gets me going so much it deserves an LTB all its own. Let's look at that one next.

CHAPTER SIX

CLIQUES SUCK

Get rid of them.

In this age of inclusivity awareness, cliques are exactly the opposite of that — they seek to *exclude* others. Nonetheless, they remain quite prevalent in today's work environments. In fact, in a 2013 study by CareerBuilder, 43 percent of employees surveyed said there were cliques in the workplace.[12] Worse yet, nearly half of those (46 percent) said their boss was part of a clique in their office.

Cliques suck the positivity, kindness, humility, and caring right out of a workplace, along with the good reputation of anyone involved, including *you*. Like I said earlier, this particular subject really gets me going.

Cliques are dangerous for a leader to be part of and just as dangerous to allow. One of the main reasons is that they are usually focused inward on the group itself rather than looking beyond their little circle to what is best for the whole team or company.

They're a tight circle, alright, and one you shouldn't have in your company at any level.

Get rid of them.

A CLIQUE IS BORN

Cliques are typically headed up by very clever people who may have perfected the art of looking great and *appearing* considerate but who, underneath the surface, are anything but. They are smart, control-hungry folks who are looking for something else entirely in the workplace besides contributing to a great company culture and supporting their teammates.

They use influence and nudging to get their hooks into people. But not just anyone. Cliques are incredibly selective as to who they want to bring into the fold. Recruits are often those having perceived power in the organization or those who will become adoring fans.

Cliques are typically passive-aggressive and influence their members as to who they should like and dislike. This one really gets my goat. It's one thing to not care for someone yourself, but it's a whole other level of mean-girl (or -guy) to encourage others to dislike someone just because they can.

I suspect this is because there's a need in them that only control can satisfy. I also suspect it doesn't really satisfy anything for more than a moment, because as soon as they onboard one person, they're off to recruit another, as if growing in number is mission-critical.

I think a particularly heinous element of a clique is how they tend to play on an employee's desire to belong. And employees need their job to support themselves and their family. When you add those two together, it's terrible to make someone feel they have to go along with a group of people in order to feel accepted so that they can keep getting their paycheck.

> I think a particularly heinous element of a clique is how they tend to play on an employee's desire to belong.

If you're in a clique... shame on you.

If you're allowing cliques... shame on you again. You should know better.

Get rid of them.

Cliques Depend on You

Cliques form, quite frankly, because they've been allowed to — by you. And don't for one minute think that the rest of the team doesn't realize you're letting this go on.

The results are far from positive. In fact, they're mostly divisive.

Some of the rest of the team will try to be part of the clique or get sucked into it, especially if the clique is getting attention and recognition despite their terrible behavior.

Others will avoid it like the plague — they want nothing to do with it, which unfortunately means the clique is likely to attack these folks by ostracizing them, or worse, planting rumors and mobilizing to get rid of the "outsider."

If you don't address these things, they will just keep going on. But no one enjoys the situation, no one grows in the end because of it, and I have never, not once, met any cliques that benefited their workplace.

Get rid of them.

They're No Dummies

Cliques don't usually consist of underperformers. To the contrary, they are typically composed of intelligent employees who make sure they perform well because they believe they can get away with bad behavior by being great at the tasks they are responsible for.

Clear as mud?

I thought so.

So let me say this — people in cliques often feel great performance is a go-pass to act badly by gossiping and excluding others. After all, they're doing their jobs, right? What could possibly be the problem?

The problem is that all that intellect might be better used to accomplish something fantastic, rather than exerting power. The other problem is that these people don't consider how well they treat others as part of their overall performance evaluation. They usually take great care to be as near to perfect as they can in the moving of the widgets, because in their mind that's all that matters.

> So let me say this — people in cliques often feel great performance is a go-pass to act badly by gossiping and excluding others.

Whether this came about in their own minds or they are modeling what they've learned elsewhere, it doesn't have any value in today's workplace. I'm not even sure it ever worked in any other period of time, for that matter.

But with a positive company culture being a must for today's rock stars, being treated badly just won't fly, and treating people badly is what cliques do best. Why should today's companies put up with this when the demand for rock stars is great, and those stars are sure to find a different company that doesn't put up with the destructive nature of a clique?

If you're not careful, the only thing flying will be the rock star you want to keep. They'll be headed someplace where they'll be happier. Someplace where there are no cliques.

See? If you're not careful, cliques can chase everyone else out. Then all you'll have left is a toxic group of people focused only on themselves.

Get rid of them.

CLIQUEY PROBLEMS

Cliques cause several problems in the workplace. They range from how the teams treat each other in the day-to-day of things, to the impact on the leaders who turn the other way.

I remember a time with an employee who I loved dearly. He was such a rock star and even great to work with. He was the rare blend of smart, fantastic personality, and kind — you know, someone everyone loved. He and I worked together for several years, and it was a joy to watch him grow. I was extremely proud.

Unfortunately, at some point he began a close connection with a clique, the head clique-r, to be exact. I hated seeing it, because I knew he'd be influenced by the group he was now hanging with; and the hub of that group was a very strong personality, much stronger than his.

It didn't take long for his demeanor to begin to change toward anyone outside of the clique. That great working relationship we'd always had diminished to almost nothing, and he began to even see me as a hindrance to his growth, despite the investment in development and even promotions I'd given him.

But what everyone else, including me, saw was that the real hindrance was the awful negativity he now surrounded himself with, which had begun to show in his own behavior. They were a small but highly negative group, and their leader had an outspoken viewpoint about, well, *everything you can imagine.* And the everything she spoke of was always bad, negative, and unfair. She knew better and more than everyone and wasn't afraid to let us all know. And she disapproved of, well, everything.

Ultimately, the employee, who had always been such a conscientious person and pleasure to work with, began to make mistakes that he would never have made before. Little things at first, and then things that required a lot of cleanup. It was so difficult to watch, and it was even more difficult to imagine how to help him get out of it, especially as he resisted anything but the briefest of connection. And he more and more began to adopt the attitude that, you guessed it, everything was bad, negative, and unfair, mirroring that head clique-r who took every opportunity to encourage that perspective.

His direct boss finally recommended that he be terminated, and I had to agree that it was the right move. We discovered that the employee had made a mistake and had never disclosed it. By the time we found the problem, it was a real mess. It took several years to straighten out in the end.

That last meeting with him was one of the hardest in my career and life. I thought the world of this young man and still do. But I also had to support the decision of his superior because we all knew it was right.

I am delighted to say, though, that it took a while, but he and I reconnected. While we haven't had the chance talk in depth about how he's doing, I do know that he found a new job that he loves, in an environment that's much more positive.

There's No "I" in Team, but There Sure Is One in "Clique"

Cliques don't place any value on the importance of being good team members, except maybe for the other members of the clique itself. They're typically there to maintain the clique itself and rarely, *very* rarely, are there to support the goals of the company. Clique members don't usually have supporting anyone outside of their group as a priority, and this is where the big disconnect between behavior and performance can lie.

For one thing, employees in a clique may not be growing and developing along with the rest of the team, which ultimately hurts the organization's culture. Clique members can be hard to coach, and it can be difficult to get them to drop these negative behaviors; they can become attached to them, especially if they're not addressed. These people remain stuck in these tendencies, a situation that doesn't support the organization's culture and can derail the positive results of having one as discussed before.

So, which came first, the cliquey chicken or the cliquey egg?

People don't form cliques simply because they aren't mentored, but they do continue the behavior because it isn't addressed. They learned it from somewhere and keep doing it because they can.

Their focus isn't on growing, except the size of the clique. They're getting something from it, some sense of influence perhaps. And sometimes they just aren't interested in changing and that can be hard to address.

Can you change them?

It's certainly worth a shot. After all, these are employees who are typically smart but have just misdirected their intelligence. Catching this tendency early enough and getting them focused on the overall mission of the team and company is a win-win.

It's hard to feel sorry for them, but the truth is that leaving these types of employees to their own devices will only hurt their careers in the end, as well as your company and team morale along the way. This usually leads, at some point, to the clique imploding into itself, or to someone finally mustering the gumption to say, "Enough."

Seriously, I can't remember one time in my career when those in the office clique didn't take a hard fall at some point. It takes a while, but sooner or later they are on the outs because they just went too far. They can't help themselves. They push,

> **Leaving these types of employees to their own devices will only hurt their careers in the end, as well as your company and team morale along the way.**

nudge, seek to grow bigger, even get a little bolder. And then, *wham*. The whole thing blows up on them and it gets shut down.

I'll repeat — if you allow cliques to form and fester (yeah, that's the word), everyone in them will suffer ultimately in their careers.

Say, "Enough."

And then get rid of them.

Culture Erosion

I'm aware of instances where the damage caused by cliques tears down entire corporate cultures. It's no small thing. Companies these days work hard to build a culture where employees thrive, and as discussed earlier, culture is more important than ever these days. After all, that great talent you want in your company pays attention to the culture of a company. They're picky about where they want to work, and they should be.

If a company has a culture issue, great talent will find out about it and then shy away from joining. Plus, the great talent currently employed there is likely to leave for something, and some*where*, better.

Since cliques often operate by exclusion and bullying, they can rapidly take a great culture and essentially break it down to one where mistreatment of each other is allowed.

Nobody likes that, and nobody finds it fun to work under those conditions, except maybe the very few in the clique itself. Until it blows up on them, that is.

So Long, Trust

I've also heard about a few leaders who permit cliques to operate. This typically backfires, ultimately seriously tearing down their own reputation as a leader with everyone else in the company. The kicker is that those not in the clique typically far outnumber the head count in the clique itself.

That right there is something to think about, isn't it?

Giving attention or leeway to a small group either because you don't have time to deal with it or maybe because they are good at moving the widgets will only result in the complete loss of trust and enthusiasm of everyone else who sees it — plus everyone else they tell about it.

Wow. Read that again.

If the clique is in charge, you won't like what happens next. Which is...

... No Free Thinking Allowed

Cliques rely heavily on groupthink, defined by *Psychology Today* as a "phenomenon that occurs when a group of well-intentioned people makes irrational or non-optimal decisions spurred by the urge to conform or the belief that dissent is impossible."[13]

That sounds about right.

To maintain their group, those at the helm of a clique must exert a level of influence over the members. This is typically accomplished by making others feel like they must go along with whatever the members say or feel. It's a power move, and one that is usually successful when there's a strong personality ruling the roost over others who are a bit more passive.

When the clique rules the thinking, what results is a lack of that wild thinking I spoke about earlier. No one is focusing on moving the business forward or creating cool new things to sell. They're instead focused on staying in the clique and not doing something that would get them pushed out of the group.

It's even worse when the team leader is perceived as having given their blessing to the clique or as being a part of it. Now the members are fearful for their jobs because getting sideways with the clique might mean their jobs are in jeopardy, at least in their minds.

After all, a culture full of cliques is not a safe one for airing one's thoughts freely.

Can You Say Bullies?

People in cliques are bullies. Boy, that does feel good to say out loud (even in print). I'll just bet there are a lot of employees out there, including the ones on your team, who would agree. Some of them might even be cheering right now.

Everyone except the ones in a clique, that is.

But make no mistake, everyone in a clique is perceived as a bully — and that includes the leader if they're part of it or appear to be, or if it looks like they support it or passively let it happen.

Let's go with D, all of the above.

Get rid of them.

HOW TO AVOID BECOMING CLIQUE BAIT

One of the best ways to eliminate a clique and the massive damage it can cause is to make sure its members understand a new definition of "mistake." That being that gossip or involvement in a clique is a mistake equal to a serious foul-up of any other kind.

Equal. As in, the same.

I recommend tying this type of behavior to a performance review, a salary review, or promotion opportunities. It could be as simple as a line item on the employee's review titled "Team Morale and Productivity," with a place for you to evaluate it. This could further provide a place to evaluate and comment on the employee's level of engagement and fairness, even inclusivity, with others they need to collaborate with on a regular basis.

Or go a step further and perform an annual survey of their team, asking them to comment or rate their leader on what they've done well and what they could improve on. Areas for this might include clarity of goals, support in their growth, training opportunities, how they're coached, etc.

Even if their members are brilliant, cliques are way too costly, and you'd be better off with someone far more brilliant in how they genuinely *treat* folks, than in how incredible they are at moving the widgets.

And since clique members are usually smart, they'll quickly understand the tie between their own performance review and their team's evaluation of how they're being led. And the people who never got sucked into it will be ever so grateful to you for taking this action.

Then, give them a chance to change.

Just one.

And if they don't, I think you can guess my last words on the subject.

Get rid of them.

CHAPTER SEVEN

DON'T CALL THEM FAMILY UNLESS YOU MEAN IT

They may believe you.

It's popular nowadays for companies to refer to their teams as family. It's a wonderful thought and sounds super nice, after all. It even has a ring of belonging to it, and we all want that, right?

But it can be *super* problematic too.

I recently came across a post on reddit.com by someone who told of his experience with a former employer that had always called the employees a family. The writer said the CEO and COO had always made it a point to know their team, including their spouses and kids, among other things, and had even visited this man when his child was sick. People stayed on at the company, many for decades.

Then one day he walked in and was told his position was eliminated. He was handed some severance, was asked for his company car keys, and that was that. He didn't even have a ride home when the car was taken, which was bad enough. But worse, neither the CEO nor the COO ever said a word to him again. I can imagine that what went through his mind was something like, "So much for family."

He went on to say that he felt he had been seen as family only as long as they needed him, "but never be mistaken that they won't walk your ass out the door in a heartbeat" if they need to for economic reasons.

To be fair, I think most companies and leaders who refer to their teams and companies as a family genuinely mean well. It's a nice sentiment and attractive to most. The employees, like the leaders saying it, want to feel the sense of camaraderie, loyalty, and trust that comes from being a family, challenges and all. That's got some heart in it, I admit. That heart tug, however, is also part of the problem.

In a recent *Harvard Business Review* article, Joshua Luna wrote that calling your team or company a family is "one of the biggest organizational mistakes I see among managers and high-performing teams."[14] The article also discusses research suggesting positive results from the practice, such as increased loyalty. But there is a flip side, which includes a tendency toward unethical behavior where the loyalty translates into not reporting wrongdoing or blurring the lines to protect the "family." This, along with other factors, including pressure to do their part, can result in burnout, attrition, and losses in productivity, Luna wrote.

ALL IN THE FAMILY?

So, let's be real: A workplace team is not quite the same as a family. It's just not. When you call your team a "family," it can often bring with it a few unspoken promises that you may just not be able to keep, but your team probably expects.

For one thing, "family" means different things to different people. For some it conveys a sense of permanence. After all, despite how family members can act at times, for the most part, we still love them and stand by them — they're still family, right? We may not look forward to turkey every year with them, but we show up and love 'em. Why? Because we're *family*, that's why.

> When you call your team a "family," it can often bring with it a few unspoken promises that you may just not be able to keep, but your team probably expects.

But with work teams, try as we might to keep together, we will part ways with them at some point. It's not a permanent group. Either they will leave, or we will need to help them leave for a variety of reasons.

Furthermore, while some employees may thrive in this type of close environment, some may want more privacy. Organizational familism, as it's often called, can create emotional attachments that aren't always positive, and can lead to a culture where teammates are seen as brothers and sisters instead of colleagues. This can give the impression that they're required to be very open about their personal business, lives, thoughts, and more. While some are open to that type of connection with others, there are just as many who are not.

For instance, while some people have experienced their families as close and bonding, many others' families were not as warm. Worse, an employee may have had a difficult childhood with their family. When the familial experience is not close, calling your team a family can conjure up memories of something they don't want any part of. This may make them naturally aloof and disconnected.

Calling your team a family can also imply, whether intentional or not, that more loyalty and transparency are given (and expected) than many people are okay with. It can inadvertently imply that they are expected to go above and beyond, just as they might at home. And if you're not careful, pushing the issue of being a family can morph into an "our way or the highway" feeling to the rest of the team, which can feel like being pressured to be part of a giant clique.

WHAT'S WRONG WITH "TEAM" ANYWAY?

When did "team" become a bad word? It didn't. So why not just use it?

It's used for nearly every sport out there, and it seems to work for them just fine. In fact, I know of and have read about companies that use this "sports" approach to pull people together to form happy, productive teams. They *are* a team — like a sports team — focused on the same goals, but understanding that sometimes players, or rather members, leave.

And with that understanding up front, there's bound to be far less of the expectation of permanence than if they think they're a family. It takes away the fear that some may have of trying to be this or that family member and turns the focus to being a great team player and member.

Teams and larger organizational communities are typically focused on a shared purpose, coming together to accomplish something great. Isn't this what you want them to accomplish anyway?

News flash: It's what they want too.

Use of the word "team" or "community" can make for a healthy culture of growth, empathy, belonging, and a feeling of being valued by leadership and teammates alike. Even the term "tribe" is often used by companies, but it does come with a word of caution, as "tribe" can be synonymous with "family" for many people. Members of a true tribe are generally born into it, and their membership lasts a lifetime.

Finding the term that best suits your organization, and clearly defining its meaning, is what's important. Doing so can bring a group together, providing a healthy sense of belonging for everyone but rarely, if ever, crossing the emotional boundaries that some may feel when called a family.

WHAT IF YOU STILL CHOOSE TO CALL THEM FAMILY?

It's not impossible to successfully continue calling your team a family as long as you avoid some pitfalls. It does take work, though.

One thing is certain: For your team to believe this, you must see it through as best you can. Applying the family sentiment unfairly or inconsistently can backfire. To decide whether this will work for the whole team, think about how you'd handle some different situations.

Finding the Right People

First off, the single most important step is ensuring you get the right folks on board so you can avoid a lot of problems that the wrong folks bring with them.

Personally, I don't think leaders, or companies in general for that matter, take nearly the time that should be taken in finding the right folks to join their team. This starts with really figuring out who best fits in, and who will not only thrive and contribute, but grow and add to the right energy and culture of the team and company now, as well as 10 years down the line.

If you're going to call your team a family, this means you'll want to look for people who will feel comfortable and thrive in that kind of group. Some people who prefer to keep their professional relationships at a more distanced level will not be comfortable in this kind of atmosphere, and there's nothing wrong with either perspective. But they should know what they're getting into, and so should you.

Really digging into finding the right people also results in less turnover and associated costs, less disruption to workflow and productivity, and fewer hits on the morale of the group.

Think about the rock stars on your team now who are great at what they do and represent what you and your company need today and what you're growing into.

Then, hire more of those folks.

Keep in mind this isn't about hiring everyone who's exactly alike, either. They may share your values, but their beautiful diversity, and how it works together and paves the way for all the different perspectives, talents, and innovation that come with it, is also vital.

It's really that simple.

Be Mindful During Terminations and Resignations

Real family, for most people, is forever. Work family, as mentioned, is not. In fact, groups at work are destined to *not* be together forever. That's just the nature of work. People move on. Sometimes they move on because they decide to and sometimes because you've decided they have to.

If you've been calling employees family since they came into your organization, you have to treat them that way going out.

A departure and how it's handled is something your team pays a lot of attention to, and so should you. They watch closely how you treat someone who is leaving and what you say afterward, as well as how you allow them to be treated by others.

> If you've been calling employees family since they came into your organization, you have to treat them that way going out.

Make sure that your behavior in this case aligns with what you say you believe in, the culture you support in the organization. Also, ensure you don't tolerate any less from anyone else.

Situations like terminations or resignations are fraught with emotion, especially if the employees have been told for some time that they're a family. The whole team may feel like they're losing someone they genuinely love. With that comes all the emotion you can imagine, from sadness and hurt to shock and lack of understanding to downright anger.

So, don't underestimate the depth of these emotions for your team and how they view these situations. Although it's not true in every case, the departing employee has probably worked closely with the rest of the team, and they may have a relationship that is closer than you know.

Termination Meetings Send a Message

For a leader, a termination meeting is typically their last opportunity to show kindness and integrity to the person leaving. Blow that, including how you act afterward, and it sends a terrible message to your team.

Even if the termination is justified, for the person leaving, after having been told they were "family" for years, two things can happen in their minds: (1) you are suddenly no longer treating them like family and (2) they believe you were faking this "family" stuff all along (and so may the rest of the team still with you).

Take care to handle their departure in the way that is in alignment with the "family" culture you have been telling them about. If the person actually was family, would you change how you treat them? Probably. So be aware that how you treat them is closely watched by everyone else. If you don't treat them well as they leave, everyone will now believe the family message was nothing but fake news.

Offer Outplacement Help

Help for those departing is something to try, and it's a solid win-win. Not only does it show caring and concern for the person leaving, but they are likely to find another position sooner. Plus, it's just the right thing to do if at all possible, providing that gross misconduct is not the reason for the termination.

There are companies that offer outplacement services, which include help with résumé writing, interviewing, and more. These services are easy to find and well worth the cost.

Think about What Happens after They Leave

Remember: If your employees have bonded under the label of "family" and one leaves, at least some of your remaining team will probably continue interacting with the one who left. After all, family is family, right?

This brings up an important point: Never, I repeat never, tell the employees left behind not to contact the person who just left. If you've been telling them they're all family for a while, suddenly telling them they have to cut contact will not go over well. Besides, they're likely to start dialing the phone less than one nanosecond after you give this command, anyway.

I'm reminded of a story a friend told me about his company from a few years back. A manager was terminated at the company, and within a few days, a far lesser-experienced manager was promoted to replace him.

This didn't look great to the team there, but it looked even worse when the new manager told some on the team not to contact the previous manager.

The team had been remarkably close to that manager. He had taught them and helped them grow — cared for them a great deal. Their "family" had just been ripped apart, and now they weren't supposed to contact a former member.

Why do that? While the incoming manager may have had his reasons, to the team, it seemed that he was simply being a bit of a jerk, and a heartless one at that. Plus, they were pretty ticked about being told who they could call.

And, you guessed it, they all started calling their former boss immediately.

So, here's what that boiled down to in the eyes of the team. First, it was in sharp contrast to how they'd been told employees were valued and treated at work. Second, a ton of fear moved in — fear about saying anything to anyone; fear that if they did reach out to their former manager, they'd be fired next; and fear that everything they'd believed about their workplace being a family was suddenly a lie.

Total mess, all right.

Don't fall into the trap of thinking you can minimize the impact of someone leaving by also trying to control people outside work. Your team does not feel that's your place at all, even if you feel it's best for them. Plus, now you've made it extra spicy.

Leave it be. If you've built a foundation of trust, they'll come around. If you haven't — better get moving on that.

WHATEVER YOU DECIDE, WALK THE WALK

Whether you've decided to call the team a family or not, your organization's culture will always require some attention and work. It's like the gas tank of your car: You have to fill it up now and then or it just quits running. Bonds and relationships form in the workplace, some long term, and these don't end the moment someone's place on the team does.

The effort includes what you do and say, day in and day out, and making sure that it's all in alignment with whatever word you choose to describe the team. You'll have to be in alignment with it and set the tone all the time — as in 100 percent. That includes leading from that spirit and making decisions from it as well.

So, whether you call them family, community, tribe, or team, remember you are modeling that decision with your every action and word. This includes what you allow others to get away with, what that means to you, and what you expect from them.

Whether the team members meet that expectation or are growing into it, they still expect *you* to meet it every day, including and beyond the day they (and their teammates) move on.

CHAPTER EIGHT

IF YOU SHOW PEOPLE YOU DO OR DON'T CARE, THEY'LL RETURN THE FAVOR

It's the Golden Rule of Leadership.

What you put into your team is generally what they'll give back. It's just the nature of humans, and the work relationship between leader and employee is no different.

When a team feels appreciated and valued, that they matter and their contribution counts, they generally give that energy and effort right back. This goes both ways, however. Treat them poorly, and they'll return that too.

Just to be clear, though, expecting 100 percent effort and the corresponding results from your team is different from what you expect from your own 100 percent and your results. It's important to remember that.

Keep in mind that they're not you. They're still learning. As their leader, you're likely a bit more skilled and experienced and so, honestly, your 100 percent *should* be different.

You should probably keep that in mind too.

YOU GET WHAT YOU GIVE

You may have heard the old saying "you get what you give." It's the same thing with leadership — how you treat your team, inspire them, and give them time and attention. If you're giving them what they need, they'll give it right back to you and to the company you're trying to grow. And it goes both ways: If you do the opposite, you'll get the opposite.

Think about that for a minute.

Any situations coming to mind? How about situations you wished you'd handled a little better? I know I have more than a few — things and circumstances where I wished I'd given more or maybe backed off a little. There are a few where I wished my own manager had handled the situation differently. But, hey, it's easy to Monday-morning-quarterback all of that. As a leader, though, take the lesson and move forward, and do better than you did before.

I was working at a large company many years ago, and our department manager called a meeting. I honestly don't re-member why he called it, but he was obviously ticked off about something based on the way he called us in. That part I remember very well.

There we were, all gathered, looking at each other nervously and hoping to glean some idea of what this was all about from each other's faces. If anyone knew something, nobody was giving it up.

The boss walked over with a quick, determined pace that always took on a light stomp when he wasn't happy about something. We knew the pace, and we knew the stomp. We paid attention, all right.

Worse yet, he was looking straight ahead as he walked. It was almost as if he was saying, "I'm mad at *all* of you, so I'm not making eye contact with any of you."

Uh-oh, something definitely was *UP*. Everything about his body language, his posture, and his tight jaw told us that there was a problem, and that we were part of it.

He joined our impromptu circle and almost quietly, but with a certain sting, said, "I've heard that some of you are talking about how I'm handling things." He continued, "I'm here to tell you that I don't give a *damn* what you think about what I do or how I do it. Just do *your* job."

And with that, he stormed away, still lightly stomping, and still looking ahead defiantly. And still angry.

Huh?

I had no idea what he was referring to. Whatever it was, I hadn't been part of it — at least I didn't think I had. But I felt like I'd been punished anyway, and so did everyone there that day. I'll bet we were all wondering who that little bugger was that created this mess.

I still have no idea all this time later what had happened, or why, for whatever reason, the manager had chosen to lay it on everyone as he did.

I felt it was such a huge mistake on his part to treat us like that. Plus, it was in very sharp contrast to the personality we'd seen in him all along. This is sort of an ode to the Don't Lose Your Sh*t Truth Bomb, but he didn't look funny at all. Nothing was funny.

We were all scared to do anything further, because he'd treated us as if we'd all been part of the problem and none of us mattered. We were frightened and unsure — *not* thinking about work at all, and definitely not in his fan club anymore.

He lost his entire team's trust and loyalty in the 30 seconds it took for him to say those words to us. And he let us all know, maybe even without meaning to, that we didn't matter to him. True or not, his message was perceived as saying we were just mindless widget movers.

Message received.

The disdain and disrespect the boss had treated us with were exactly what he got back from us for a long time after. Maybe not to his face, mind you, but I assure you the undercurrent was electric with contempt. No one forgot that moment. He didn't give a damn what we thought. So we stopped giving a damn what he thought, too.

In fact, several of us, including me, left shortly after that.

An employee treated in this way is not going to be gung ho about doing the best job possible and making big things happen for quite a while.

Just imagine what opportunities for business growth and cool stuff were missed while we all focused instead on the eggshells we were walking on. For some time after the event, we all avoided this manager and didn't dare seek opportunities to chat about new ideas and thoughts. Those could have been great ideas but instead were pushed down to avoid another tongue lashing. And there's the energy spent on worrying about the situation. All that energy could have instead gone into thinking of those new ideas or even getting things done.

The previous story shows one way a leader can respond when their expectations aren't met. We've talked about a lot of situations like that, but in this LTB, let's look a little harder at what kind of expectations we as leaders should have in the first place. It might just be that we can avoid a lot of this disappointment entirely by a little change of thinking.

SETTING EXPECTATIONS

For a leader, setting expectations can be tricky sometimes because you also want to be fair. On one hand, you want to let people know they have a chance to learn and grow, so they need to feel safer to make mistakes. But on the other hand, everyone has a job to do, and they should be getting results for the company at some point. They key is to remember how your own actions fit with the actions of the team.

Setting High Expectations Includes Having Patience

You must keep in mind that, in most cases, your team does not own the business. They're not there just for the organization; they're there for their own growth and to support themselves and their loved ones. And they probably aren't in leadership roles — yet, anyway. If they are, I'm guessing they're at a junior level to your role, since they are your direct reports.

In short, they may not be where you are mentally or with the same developed skills that come with time and experience.

Having the expectation that they will work as hard as you do, or at your level, may not be realistic. Having the expectation that they will do their best and learn along the way is, however, realistic. But that's not likely to happen unless you're leading them well and inspiring them to do that.

I don't mean "carrot and stick" inspiration — true inspiration comes from and lives in the heart. It's the kind that keeps the team motivated and feeling excited to contribute even when you're not around.

It's your job to inspire them to feel they're a part of the vision, and to feel they have ownership of their role and understand its importance in the overall mission. If you are inspired and take ownership, you will model that for them, and they will start doing it, too. So you have to walk your talk — otherwise, your team will be all talk, too. And then nothing will get done. You can't set high expectations for them but not for yourself.

You work for them as their leader in this way, and it's what they are looking for in you.

Be Consistent with What You Tolerate

What happens when no matter what you do, someone isn't performing?

Tolerating an underperformer is just as bad as having too high of expectations. It can have a terrible effect on your team. It's essentially telling them you don't expect much from the employee who is not performing well, but you still expect more from everyone else. Teams find this incredibly unfair, and I have to say I agree with them.

It's equally uncaring to the person you're keeping around who is struggling. They're probably miserable too and highly aware that they aren't cutting it. They are likely struggling and know it, and everyday pings them just a bit harder with the reminder that they aren't making the grade.

There's a quote by marketing expert Perry Belcher that comes to mind on this topic: "Nothing will kill a great employee faster than watching you tolerate a bad one."

Amen, Perry.

Having different standards, or levels of quality, will definitely kill morale and any sense of ownership and enthusiasm that your team has about their work. Why work as hard if it doesn't count? Why try harder than Sally if it gets me nowhere?

Why, indeed.

Would you be able to answer that latter question if Sally was an underperformer on your team?

While each team member is different and may need different things from you than others do, the standards of quality should be consistent. And the employees should all be expected to perform to those standards within their own role. You cannot expect some to continuously outperform someone else who is not pulling their own respective weight.

THE GOLDEN RULE IS EVERYWHERE (OR SHOULD BE)

The thing about the Golden Rule is that we tend to apply it only at certain times or places. We haven't really considered it as part of our work lives.

Why is this?

One strong reason is that the Golden Rule is pretty much based on feelings and how to treat people. When you seek to detach feelings from the workplace, it would follow that something based on them would be diminished as well. Through the decades, businesses have done that, as mentioned before, but now that's changing. Employees are seeking workplace cultures that support a sense of caring and giving, and this is right up the Golden Rule's alley.

Author Steve Farber has a way of addressing this mentality the best, and it goes something like this: "Nowhere does the Golden Rule apply only Monday through Friday, between the hours of 9:00 a.m. and 5:00 p.m."[15]

That Steve is pretty smart too.

And he's right.

The Golden Rule is about our very own humanness. But somehow, we decided that to be truly professional we have to walk around as though we're made of cardboard.

A Common Thread

It's silly to think that in order to succeed at leading a group of people, we have to lose our humanness and forget things like "do unto others" that many of us hold so dear in our faith.

And by "many of us," I mean a lot of people. Millions, in a lot of religions. Eight that I could find.

Don't believe me? Here they are:[16]

- **Christianity:** "So in everything, do to others what you would have them do to you, for this sums up the Law and the Prophets." —Matthew 7:12 (NIV)[17]
- **Islam:** "The Prophet Muhammad said, 'None of you will have faith till he wishes for his (Muslim) brother what he likes for himself.'" —[Al-Bukhari], Hadith 13[18]
- **Judaism:** "What is hateful to you, do not to your neighbour: that is the whole Torah, while the rest is the commentary thereof; go and learn it." —*The Complete Babylonian Talmud*[19]
- **Baha'I:** "Choose thou for thy neighbor that which thou choosest for thyself." —Baha'u'llah, Baha'i prophet[20]
- **Hinduism:** "One should never do that to another which one regards as injurious to one's own self." —Mahabharata (113)[21]
- **Buddhism:** "Look where you will, there is nothing dearer to man than himself; therefore, as it is the same thing that is dear to you and to others, hurt not others with what pains yourself." —Udanavarga 5:18[22]
- **Daoism:** "Regard your neighbor's gain as your own gain, and your neighbor's loss as your own loss." —T'ai Shang Kan Ying P'ien[23]
- **Confucianism:** "Zigong asked, 'Is there a single word that can serve as the guide to conduct throughout one's life?' The Master said, 'It is perhaps the word "shu." Do not impose on others what you yourself do not want [others to impose on you].'" —The Analects (15:24)[24]

And just in case you're wondering, beyond religion, the great minds and philosophers of years gone by seem to have agreed with the concept of the Golden Rule. Here are just a few:

- **Plato (428–347 BCE):** "Do to others as you want others to do to you."[25]
- **Thales of Miletus (c. 624–546 BCE):** "Avoid doing what you would blame others for doing."[26]
- **Isocrates (436–338 BCE):** "Do not do to others that which angers you when they do it to you."[27]

I'll just bet these religions and philosophers speak to the hearts of many people throughout this big, beautiful, diverse world. The various religions and cultures that exist may be different in how they view things, but they all have a common thread showing how we should treat each other.

I'd say there's a message in there for all of us — religion and philosophy aside. How we treat each other matters, and it matters a great deal.

It sure matters to your team.

Treat them well, believe in them, and they will return the favor time and time again in how they work with their heart and how they walk through the door at work every day.

Feels nice just saying it.

HOW TO SHOW YOU CARE

It's easy to say, "Show you care," but there's no single way to do it. Each day in a workplace can have its own issues, and team members all have different personalities — as they should, right?

So, there's no one best way to let people know that you care. However, there are many ways you can let them know.

It's about finding what works for this person or that one, and that's where knowing your team comes in real handy. Caring comes from the heart, which is something you just kinda feel, when you're giving it and receiving it…. You know — that personal stuff again.

The best way to show your team that you care is, well, to really *CARE*.

Why is this hard for some leaders to do? Are you someone who has trouble with this?

The answer may be as mentioned before — it's not been the norm. Plus, leaders traditionally have not been taught to bring a sense of caring into work. The lack of teaching in this area could be because of legitimate fears over misunderstandings. What's the proper way to show you care without it feeling intrusive to the recipient? Misunderstandings can even lead to claims of harassment and other sticky (and costly) legal situations. It can therefore seem much easier, and feel safer, to just hold back rather than risk stepping over a line that may not always be clear to everyone involved.

Nearly every company today has (or should have) policies around harassment, and everyone should know them *and* follow them. Clarity is definitely key in this aspect to avoid that legal hot water.

However, genuine, heartfelt caring always respects boundaries. It's mainly about showing your team that you are invested in them and their growth by taking the time to talk with them about it; paying attention to it, to what they need in order to take those steps; and then helping them make those moves. The more everyone understands each other, the less chance you have of being misunderstood or of accidentally violating a boundary.

Caring also means always celebrating those steps when taken and all the wins along the way.

So ask yourself some questions: *Do I care about these people? Or am I just here to do a job? If I'm just here to do a job... is this the right job for me? How can I lead if I don't care about my team?*

I'm guessing your answer will be that you do care, or you wouldn't still be reading this book. So, next questions....

If I do care, is anything getting in the way of my communicating that? How has the team been reacting to me? Do they know I care?

How can I show it better? What things do I need to change? What would each of my team members appreciate — and would the things one person would choose differ from what another would want? How? And why?

Now do the other important thing: Go ask them. And listen to what they tell you.

The good news is that after you start thinking this way, caring isn't as hard. Feeling something is in our nature. Caring comes in by way of being aware of feelings, yours and your teams', and then showing it with words, attention, listening, kindness, etc.

Even in the moments when something has gone wrong and you have to correct an employee, having your message come from a place of caring can diffuse or reshape it to be more impactful and encouraging.

I had a boss once who had a way of telling me I'd done something wrong in such a way that I wasn't belittled one bit. He was so good at it that I actually felt encouraged after the meeting. I often joked with him that he was the only person I'd ever known who told me I'd done something wrong and I felt like a million bucks afterward.

How did he do that?

He cared. Even when he was telling me I'd made a boo-boo, the fact that I was important and that he believed in me came through. I knew I had to fix something, and not do it again, but he believed that I could. My focus was on that, doing better, instead of getting stuck on the error. His way of coaching and guiding me, even in the time he had to redirect me, told me he knew I could. That was where he was focused.

He was right. I could do better. And I did.

CHAPTER NINE

HIRE GREAT PEOPLE, THEN GET OUT OF THEIR WAY

Give them some room to learn.

They'll mess up sometimes. So what?

Didn't you make mistakes when you were growing?

KIDS, THEY SAY THE DARNDEST THINGS

My daughter inspired this Leadership Truth Bomb years ago. I raised her as a single mom and wanted the best for her. I was not the best mom, but I tried hard. Being the overachiever I am, I figured I would just do as much as I could, as often as I could, and it would be the right thing to do. I'd be some sort of supermom.

When she was growing up and would get into the smallest amount of trouble or need help, I would swoop in mamabear style and take care of it. That's what I should do, right? Show her that I was *always* there, *always* willing to do whatever I needed to do to make her life easier — *always*.

I was showing her how much I loved her, how much family could, and should, depend on each other. I'd clean up situations and problems quickly, efficiently, and whenever needed. Boom; done.

One day when my daughter was in her early twenties, she asked to talk with me. She seemed quite serious, and my head immediately began to swirl with the possibilities — dinged the car, lost her wallet, had an argument with someone, made a bad grade, someone was mean to her.... I was already grabbing my purse, ready to spring into action and save the day.

But instead, what she had to say rocked me to my core way more than any of those things I was thinking. And what she gave me that day is one of the best leadership lessons I've ever received.

"Mom," she said, "when you jump in and take care of everything for me, it makes me feel like you don't think I'm capable."

I responded, or rather *didn't*, with stunned silence.

Imagine my combination of shock, pride in what she was saying, and hurt — not in that she'd said it, but in that she was right. Damn, damn.

I thought I had been doing the right thing all this time, teaching her to always be there for the ones we love. But what I'd actually taught her was that I didn't believe in her.

I'll wait here if you need to go back and read that story again.

It's a perfect example of thinking you're doing one thing but accomplishing the very opposite. I was doing what I thought was best but hadn't bothered to consider her perception at all. She *wanted* to stumble a little, and she wasn't afraid to because *she* believed in herself; she just didn't think I believed in her.

Kids. They really do say the darndest things.

I love this story because it made me immediately think about how I interacted with others and how I was leading my team. Was I a "helicopter leader"? Clearly, I'd been buzzing around as a mom, but did I take that approach into work too with my team? I'm sure I did, maybe still do. But bringing awareness around this helped me notice and avoid most of these moves.

I literally get applause when I say this one out loud in a speaking or training engagement. Your team would put this Truth Bomb near, if not at, the top of what they want you to know. They don't mind learning and even hearing they got something wrong. What they *do* mind is you never giving them the chance to spread their wings. They mind you not letting them grow, even if that means failing a little and trying again.

> **Sometimes, as leaders, we just need to butt out. Period.**

There's just no other way to say it.

Sometimes, as leaders, we just need to butt out. Period.

DELEGATING IS TEACHING

I get it. You can't always do that with highly important tasks. I mean, Johnny isn't going to be allowed to do a complicated brain surgery by himself the day after he graduates from medical school, right?

But if you don't find a way to gauge the talent and skill development, Johnny is never going to be able to do it all. Do you plan to do it all yourself forever? No? Well, better let Johnny get up to speed.

Delegating is teaching. Getting out of their way is showing trust, yes, but it's also showing that you notice their potential and value, and that you believe they can do a thing.

If you never delegate, *you* will never grow either (nor will your company). Delegating frees you up to do more and helps drive the business forward. It stretches you as a leader and it stretches your team to try on new things and improve. Yes, they will mess up. That's part of the process. But if you've prepared them well, they will be able to take on more and grow.

They win. You win. That's what you're there to do — to develop and grow your team.

If you aren't able to do that, you'll never teach them how to be a leader who delegates. Further, your ability to grow in your own leadership will be stifled.

If you have a tendency to hoard work and responsibilities, particularly things that your team should be able to take on, why? Not enough time to explain things? Why is that? Not willing to let it go? Why is that? Don't trust others' judgment? What's with that?

Feel you can do it better, quicker, the right way, etc. etc.? Drop that for *sure*.

The alternative to delegating and teaching them is that you do it F.O.R.E.V.E.R.

Is that really what you want? I would hope not.

So let them stumble now and then. Catch them, help them when they need it, but let them breathe a little. The more you trust them, the less afraid they'll be to try, and the more confident they'll be in trying something new.

They'll be focused on applying all that they've learned versus proving they're worthy of giving it a go.

> **They'll be focused on applying all that they've learned versus proving they're worthy of giving it a go.**

DON'T CUT OTHER LEADERS OFF AT THE KNEES

There used to be an old toy commercial that said, "Weebles wobble but they don't fall down."

Weebles were a toy introduced in 1971 by Hasbro.[28] Each figure had a rounded bottom with a weight in it. You could push it as hard as you wanted, and it would wobble back and forth but never topple over. Turns out, to my surprise, Weebles are still around (now considered "vintage"; should have hung onto mine), and now mimic today's popular characters for toddlers.

Just as Weebles won't fall down, neither will your team, which may include leaders who report to you with teams of their own. Just as you need to let your own team wobble a bit, you need to let other leaders wobble, too.

You simply must *never* get in between your direct reports and their own teams. Unless something awful is going on, getting in the middle is a recipe for disaster — yours included.

I had a situation in my career moons ago that speaks to this issue and the damage it causes. I would start a new project with my direct reports, only to find out from them later that my boss had gone directly to them and made a change. Once, a significant change was even announced in a full meeting with one of my employees right there by her side. I could feel everyone's thoughts shoot my way. Though humiliated, I tried to maintain my composure even as my face turned red from embarrassment.

I don't know who was more uncomfortable by her actions, my team or me. Clearly, we all felt awkward when it happened, and I had the bonus of being horrified and belittled. As a result, I began to question my ability and to wonder why on earth I remained there if I couldn't be trusted with the tiniest of things. I mean, I had all the credentials, the education, the experience — didn't those count? Isn't this what she hired me for?

I wrestled with those thoughts and feelings until I realized she did it to nearly everyone.

Everyone. And they all felt the same way.

Why You Should Stay Out of the Middle

It's tempting, I know, to want to step in, like I did for my daughter all those years ago, and I wouldn't be honest if I said I never did it to my team. You might think you're just helping them out, that they'll be so appreciative and learn something.

But what actually happens is very different.

Your direct reports who are leaders can't stand it.

Their teams are confused by it (and also can't stand it).

The leaders feel just like my daughter did. *Believe that I can do it,* they're likely to think. Or, worse, *Why* don't *you believe in me?* followed sometime later by, *Forget this noise; I just won't do anything then,* and finally the worst, *I'm outta here.*

If you do wedge yourself in between your direct reports and their own teams, you will cause a number of problems.

First, as I said previously, you will confuse the heck out of their team. They have a leader, yet the boss one step up is telling them what to do. Now I'm not saying don't interact with them — absolutely be available and chat them up. But when you start going behind the back of their own leader (which is how they will see it), even with the best of intentions, you put the employees between a rock and a hard place.

They don't know what they should do. They have a boss telling them one thing, and now the boss's boss is telling them something different.

Goodness... how do they stay out of trouble here?

Listening to one and not the other is going against the grain of one of them.

So, who do they choose? How do they choose? The biggest boss? The one closest to them?

You see the mess it creates.

I'll add this: If you do this to your own team members who are leaders, they are completely humiliated, and it undermines their leadership with their own team. You are essentially telling them you don't trust or believe in them or want them making any decisions.

And if you don't trust them, why should their own team?

DON'T BE A SWOOPER

Are you a swooper?

A swooper is a leader who puts their team in charge of something and then swoops in at the last minute, right before a project or task is finalized, and starts changing everything. These are leaders who take a day or week off (although RARELY) and upon returning fresh and raring to go, start going through everything possible to find what was missed.

Swoopers tend to be perfectionists, which is a whole other subject I may write a book on. They have a very hard time letting go of anything, so delegation is pretty much out the window.

Somehow, they became convinced that they have the right way, the only way, and the best timing, and no one can possibly ever do it as well as them.

The problem is that swooping is a total morale killer for your team and will stop productivity in a New York minute (or the minute of whatever state you want to insert there).

Your team really dislikes it when you swoop. They probably start mentally and emotionally preparing themselves right before a project launch or your return from vacation. They may begin running through every step or checklist, dreading the coming episode of you pointing out all that they've missed. Even if you don't find anything wrong, the team might be relieved, but look at all the energy they've just wasted.

And then there's the Ninja Swooper (*insert ninja sound*): "Let's change a few things at the *last minute*." You know the type. Are *you* the type?

If you are, uh-oh. To your team, it seems like you're making changes just to make them. Swooping in at the last minute can look, in your team's eyes, like you are wielding your power to turn everything upside down at the finish line, just because you can. Even if that's nowhere near the truth of your intentions.

Big ouch.

Even if the change you need to make is completely legitimate, your team may feel that you have little or no regard for the work and effort they've just put into the project or task. They feel like they wasted their time — completely.

They also feel like *you* wasted it.

They find themselves saying either, "I won't work as hard next time because she'll change everything that I did at the last minute anyway," or, "Why doesn't he just tell me everything he wants up front so that I can do it that way, instead of changing it all?"

They have a point. Why *don't* you do that?

Have Your Own Ducks in a Row First

Giving the team all that they need in order to complete something and feel accomplished is setting them up to win. If you don't have time to do that, or won't make time to do that, it's time to look at your own organizational, time management, and project-planning skills.

Speaking of project planning, there are a few things you can do at the beginning of a project to help clarify the process, smooth things out, and avoid hurt feelings and wrong perceptions:

- **Plan ahead.** Put processes, procedures, and progress reports, if warranted, in place from planning through completion and make sure everyone is aware of them. There won't be any surprises for the team along the way, and you'll have shown them a wonderful example of how to plan, and execute, a project.
- **Talk through the processes.** What things will you need to approve along the way and what triggers that process? Discuss those things.
- **Put your feedback check-ins earlier in the process.** Make your approvals easier and less disruptive to everyone involved. Even if you want to see something again just before it is finalized, if you saw it much earlier and gave clear directions, chances are it won't be nearly as offtrack as if this is the first time you're seeing it.

Then, Trust Your Team

If you don't, then take accountability for that. Ask yourself why you haven't prepared them well enough to take on something more. While you're solving those problems, you still need to train yourself to stop swooping.

Get used to watching team members Weeble and wobble, maybe even fall down a little. But pay attention to how they're growing as a result. That's the real goal anyway, and one they'll never ever forget that you helped them achieve.

There's real joy and pride in helping your team find their way. There's also some there for you in your own ability to do that.

#10

YOU HAVE A MINUTE

Yes, you do.

Make one.

Picture this: You're working furiously on a deadline that's creating mayhem for you *and* your schedule, and that deadline is rolling in in about 2.3 seconds. There might even be a little sweat on your brow, and your heart rate sounds as if you're running a 5K. Then, you hear it….

Knock, knock, knock.

"Got a minute?" asks one of your team members, standing there so very anxious to enter and start a conversation of unknown length.

Trust me, you have a minute.

You may not *want* to have one because you know it's likely to turn into 30 with this particular employee. "Oh, gosh," you think to yourself, "of all the times to want to chat, this is the *worst!*"

You don't reply right away. You're a bit twitchy with anxiety because your own boss has been *crystal* clear that things are very urgent. You are frantically checking this spreadsheet and that, Excel formulas and "IF" statements be damned, also while doing research and writing a summary for the third time — all in a blur of focus and "holy cow; I've got no time to finish this" mentality.

Sound familiar?

I think all leaders have these moments. It never fails: We just want to finish something that's got a hard due date, and right then one of our team wants to chat.

Knock, knock, knock. There it is again.

Yep, they're still there.

Remember, from your team's perspective, you're just in your office. Plus, your door is likely open to let them know how much you believe in that open-door policy you say you have. You look like you're available, even if you don't feel like you are.

And if you're really smart, you will be. So, your answer to the "got a minute" question is a simple yes.

The person wants to connect by sharing something with you — could be a neato idea or some advice they need. To get it, in their minds, all they have to do is walk in.

And they do.

And you should want them to.

That's *why* your door is open.

WHY YOU SHOULD HAVE A MINUTE

That open door. Darn it. You might be tempted to shut it in the future so you don't look available during these times.

Please don't, or at least do so very sparingly.

Keeping the flow of communication open means you remain accessible to your team, and they love this. They want to be seen, heard, valued, and listened to. If all they have to do is walk into your office for that, all the better.

Even if you can't stop right at that moment to chat with them, just the fact that they *CAN* walk in and at least get your attention for a second is huge. Remember that culture stuff we already talked about? Well, this is the way it happens. They need to know they can come and talk to you about anything, anytime.

If they feel they're a nuisance to you, you won't get all the important details you need to do your job. You need to know what's going on with the team, what they feel is important (even if you don't feel it's as important), and how their work is going. You'll get that feeling of disconnect that puts you on edge, thinking they're not telling you things you need to know. You don't want that. Neither do they.

> If they feel they're a nuisance to you, you won't get all the important details you need to do your job.

So, yes. You definitely have a minute.

MAKE THE MOST OF THAT MINUTE

Here's the catch. When someone on your team needs you, you must stop what you're doing. Even if only to acknowledge them and set a time later to chat. You must do that and convey a sense of importance on what they have to share.

And it *should* be important to you. Even if only because it's important to them.

Do the Most Important Thing First

If you can, stop and have the conversation.

If you just can't, at least give them 30 seconds to tell you what their convo request is about, and set a time on your calendar to come back to it. They know you can't necessarily drop everything, but now they're reassured that you care and you'll take time to talk when you can.

Another effective method to handle this is to keep a list handy where you can write down who needed you. Let the person see you writing their name down, and then say you'll get back to them.

But here's the trick: You have to get back to them. If you don't, they will feel you don't care, and they won't trust you the next time you try to do the same thing.

The most important thing isn't to have the conversation right then. It's to show them you care about what they want to talk about.

Put Down Your Phone

When someone is talking with you, put your phone down. Go ahead, you can do it. Just put it down.

Face down.

Turn your body and look at them... and don't try the crazy flex maneuver where your body is forward but your arms are still reaching around to one side to your keyboard so you can keep typing.

Your team knows about that one. It looks weird, but that's not the main problem. Regardless of how brilliantly talented you feel you are at multitasking, if you're working even while looking straight at them, your team feels like you don't care about them. In their minds, you're not listening; you're typing.

(And, let's be honest: You are not listening; you are, in fact, typing.)

When you turn your phone over or stop typing and just *listen*, they'll love you for that, and for valuing their input.

SPEAKING OF A MINUTE, EMAILS COUNT TOO

You have a minute to respond to emails too. Yes, you do. Maybe not right away, but you have one.

Make one. Here's why.

One of the most common complaints I've heard throughout the years from teams, including my own, is that their leader doesn't respond to emails quickly enough.

It's easy to see why, to be fair. There are a gazillion of them flying at you from all directions, and they compete with phone calls, meetings, etc. But given the digital world we live in, emails have become the new conversation. And while a quick response may not be as expected in our personal lives, at work your team does look for a quick turnaround.

Teams get very frustrated when they send an email to their leader and then have to wait a long time for the reply.

They wait.

They wait some more.

And then they start to wonder what's wrong.

They aren't sure whether their message went into a wormhole and got lost. They don't feel they can bug you by asking whether you got it, but all the while, they're asking themselves questions while waiting.

Did she get my email?

Did it go to his junk folder?

It's important, so should I go in after a while and ask her about it?

Will it tick him off if I do ask or send it again?

The second-guessing goes on and on until you *do* respond.

I know we all respond in our own way and have our own pace. But I ask you to now consider that so does your team. Generally, however, when a team member sends you an email, they really want an answer lickety-split.

They just do. They want you to know that. They probably don't realize you have a gazillion other things to complete... so they just know they are waiting.

I know it may not seem logical to you and it's not always possible to respond right then and there. After all, you can't always stop everything and respond to every email from every direction.

But your team doesn't know that. From their perspective, they've worked up the nerve to send you the email, and now they're anxiously waiting on your reply.

To help with this, it's a good idea to have guidelines in place around response times that give everyone an idea when to expect a reply, such as by end of day, or within 24 hours, etc. These might even apply only during specific times, such as during projects or other initiatives, but you'll need to say that too.

In this age of remote work, understanding when to expect a response is even more helpful to maintain engagement.

Of course, emergencies and urgent issues may need special quick attention, but define those as best you can as well — what constitutes an emergency and how best to communicate it. You might even specify that the best way to communicate in emergencies may not be through email.

Guidelines aren't an attempt to complicate things, remove yourself from the flow of communication, or close that office door (virtually or otherwise). After all, I've been talking a lot about being open and available, and that is as important as ever. This is about being clear so the team members understand turnaround times and even learn to think ahead about what they may need as they work through their day and schedule.

In the meantime, they're likely thinking, "Reply, already!" And you should. Even if to just say, "Got your email and I'll get back to you later." At least they know you got it, you saw it, and you'll get back to them.

Then do that.

Get back to them, just like you promised.

When *You're* Waiting: Give Them Another Minute

There are times when you're waiting on a reply email from your team. And waiting and waiting some more; still waiting... the minutes can seem like hours.

When you are waiting for their response, there's a temptation to charge out to your team or pick up the phone and blast a little impatience their way.

But I urge you not to.

If the problem of not getting back to you in a timely fashion isn't chronic, hold your horses just a second or two. Maybe three. Then, pull in some of that emotional intelligence we talked about earlier.

If you feel as though you must reach out to them to nudge a bit, first check that you are being realistic in your demand. This may not change the immediate need, but it can be helpful going forward to give your team a little turnaround time whenever possible. This shows you understand their time constraints too.

And with future emails, you can make sure you get the response in the time frame you need by communicating clearly. If you need something back quickly, be sure to say that in the email and consider including *why* it's urgent. That way they'll know you need it right now, or within the hour, or by end of day or whatever deadline you give, and they'll also understand the importance of their response.

Bringing clarity around general expected response times is probably the best way to make sure you get the response back when you expect it. Remember, you're modeling leadership skills to your team, and this includes setting the expectation of email responses.

TWO SMART WAYS TO MAKE SURE YOU HAVE THAT MINUTE

Dedicate Time to Email

An effective method of making sure you have time to respond quickly to emails or messages is to have a recurring time on your calendar dedicated to follow-ups via email and in person. This is a great way to avoid the stress of stopping and starting all day long, which can be exhausting.

Having a dedicated period means you are focused on the task, and you'll find it surprisingly productive for that reason alone. Plus, if your team is aware of this set time, they will know when to expect a response and will worry less about the wormhole.

Make it important — really important. Their productivity affects yours *and* the company's in general. If something is on pause waiting on a response from you, that delay may trickle uphill and affect your own deadline now, or one that's coming up soon. It may even create a new problem. Keeping a good flow of communication and response can make that "minute" even more important for completing today's work and hitting tomorrow's milestones.

Schedule and Communicate Regular Focus Time

If the need for uninterrupted, focused work time is causing you to be less responsive, consider setting those hours too. Place scheduled focus time on your calendar so that your team knows you are not available. If you can do this with your door open, all the better. But if you can't, at least they'll know why you're tucked away. If necessary, work from another place in the office, maybe a conference room or an empty office, or plan a regular work-from-home day if possible.

I think you'll be amazed at how much your team will appreciate not just the fact that you have thought this through and set some guidelines around it, but mostly that you follow those guidelines. It sends a message that you value everyone's time and contribution, and it's a huge teaching moment for them not only in the importance of communication flow, but also in following through and following up.

Give them that message — they'll never forget it.

And they'll be all the better leaders one day as a result.

#11

IT'S ABOUT THEIR GROWTH, NOT YOURS

And it's magic when it happens.

This isn't a rabbit you're pulling out of a hat, but it sure feels like it when you realize that you've helped your team grow and you've watched them succeed. I don't mean that you view them as children, but I will admit to feeling very similar to how a proud parent feels when a child conquers a learning milestone.

If you look closely, you can often see the potential in them before they do, and you know they will accomplish many things as they learn their gifts and take them for a spin.

It's your obligation as their leader to see and nurture those gifts, helping your team grow into what they can and want to be — even when they're not clear on what they can be, or what they want to become. They may just know they want *something*. If they can define it, they may not know how to go about it.

That's where you come in.

This has always been my favorite part of leadership, and I love it.

Your team depends on you to love it too.

HELPING THEM ALSO HELPS YOU

I've said it many times, but I'll say it again: It's your main responsibility as your team's leader to develop your team. That's why they're there — to learn and grow in order to be successful. This means they are looking for their purpose and finding fulfillment in that quest.

Aren't we all?

While they may care for you and look up to you, they aren't necessarily there to help YOU grow, however. They're not focused on your career — they're focused on theirs. You'll grow as a wonderful side effect of focusing on your team, I promise.

But, if you aren't going to invest into your team's development, why on earth would they stay?

They probably won't.

If you don't put the focus and investment in the team, today's rock star talent will simply move on to somewhere that does.

That means you'll lose the best, and then you'll have to find and train more of them. This

> If you don't put the focus and investment in the team, today's rock star talent will simply move on to somewhere that does.

becomes increasingly hard if the word on the street is that you don't have a path for your folks and don't see it as a priority.

The most talented workers usually have a few companies giving them a call trying to lure them away. But if they are being mentored and developed, see a path to move up in the ranks, and feel their wages are competitive, they are far less likely to answer those calls.

Believing in someone builds their confidence and shows your loyalty to them. It also gives them more reasons for building their loyalty to you as well as to the company and what you're all working to accomplish.

If you're trying to ultimately grow your business, consider that will not happen until you do the most important thing first — develop your team.

They will then naturally help you build your business.

YOU GET TO BE PART OF THEIR GROWTH

Magic. That's how it feels to love your team and support them in their growth and to see it happen. You must be in their corner, as well as in the audience, cheering them on when they're "rockin'."

If you don't have time to spend getting to know your team or figuring out how to help them grow and what they want to grow into, I have to ask, why not?

I once had to start a new department in a company, and I needed someone to head it up. But not just anyone — I needed someone with great energy, attitude, and ability to connect and deliver content in front of people in a way that was both effortless and engaging.

I knew just the person.

Let's call her Allison. She was the very definition of a rock star. The thing is, she didn't believe it. She knew she had the ability to focus and make just about anything happen. But though I and others saw this as an incredible quality in her, she didn't recognize it that way.

I met with her one day for coffee and, between sips and chatting, told her about the new department and that I thought she would be perfect for it.

"Me?" she asked, stunned, coffee cup halfway to her lips as the wheels started churning in her head.

"Oh yes, YOU," I told her, grinning. "You have everything you need for the role — energy, public speaking skills, and a genuine desire to help people; you're perfect."

"I don't know... I've never done anything like this before in my career."

I knew how she felt. After all, from her perspective, she'd never done what I was suggesting; she had never been in that particular line of work.

But that wasn't how I perceived it.

The truth was, she had all the makings of a phenomenal lead for the new team. She was high energy, very bright, and educated, and had an amazing work ethic. She was also great with people and great in *front* of people, and had successful years in another, complementary field that I knew would catapult her into this new area of work which would draw on those skills.

I could see she was nervous, but I could also see the sparkle of interest and curiosity in her eyes.

And then I asked her, "When have you ever tackled something and *not* succeeded?"

We both knew the answer. *Never.*

I have to chuckle now when I think back to that meeting. I knew without a doubt that she would be great at the new role. I just needed her belief to catch up with mine.

After thinking it over a few days, she decided to jump in. She knew I was in her corner and later told me that that made the biggest difference in her decision.

Over the coming months, I saw her transition, even Weeble and wobble. She'd come in my office, and we'd go over her questions and concerns. Most of the time, she already knew the answers; she just wanted a little assurance. But over time she needed less and less guidance as her confidence grew.

It was an easy job guiding her in her growth. It was an honor too. She has since taken on a higher role at a new company overseeing both efforts, the one she jumped into and the one she was doing before. I have zero doubt she is going to do even more.

We chat now and then, still bouncing ideas around or maybe just to say hello and catch up. Did I swell with pride? You bet. Do I still? You bet.

Like I said, magic.

WHO WILL SAY YOUR NAME?

When I'm speaking on this subject, I ask audiences to write down the name of the person or people who helped them grow, who had such a big impact on them.

It's beautiful to watch their reactions.

They instantly have a name that comes up. I can see it in their faces and in their reactions. Often there are tears as memories flood back to them, and I ask them to share about this person and what they did for them.

A lot of the stories center around someone believing in them — maybe even when others were saying they couldn't do something. Just as many are fathers, or father figures, and teachers are common. But former leaders are always in the top spots.

That's something, isn't it? Years later, folks sitting there remembering you and how you taught them — that's the impact you can have on your team.

Who did you think of when you read those last few paragraphs? Who is that person who guided you, or perhaps was unwavering in their belief in you? Write that person's name down. Better yet, pick up the phone if you can and let them know what they meant to you.

But now think about this: Who will say *your* name?

Who are you helping now?

Who will look back someday and answer this question with your name?

What would your team say if they were asked about your leadership now?

If the answers to these questions are hard to come by, you may want to rethink your approach to leadership.

WHAT THEY NEED YOU FOR

You may not realize it, but as a leader you can make a huge impact on someone's life. It sounds like a big responsibility, and it is. But it's also an opportunity that's worth it. And it will impact your life too.

Helping someone find and fulfill their purpose is not as complicated as it may sound. Just listening to them and helping them gain confidence in what they can do is a major portion of it. The rest is helping them take steps to get there.

But it all starts with you wanting to be that type of leader and knowing, down deep, that you'll fulfill your own purpose by helping them find and fulfill theirs. Keep that in mind and the rest tends to fall into place. As for "the rest," following are a few suggestions for how to approach your role.

Be Insanely Curious

I love curious people, and I've found this quality to be right up there in the top three of what to look for in new hires. Curious people are great problem solvers and innovators. They're wild thinkers and usually don't mind looking at something in a completely new way. They aren't limited by how something's always been done.

Yes, please. I'll take a whole team of them.

As a leader, you should also be insanely, ridiculously curious about each of your team members and what they need from you. Also be curious about what they're learning from you now and ask yourself whether you need to change that in some way. Then change it.

Connect with them, talk with them. Ask them. Find out what they want to do, what they're afraid of trying, what makes them tick, etc.

Then help them learn those things.

Keep an Open Mind

It's important to remain open to the fact that you may not know what your team needs from you. While I'm hoping to help you with that in this book, I also encourage you again to be sure to have *them* answer that question — they'll tell you if you just ask them. After all, they know way more than you do about it.

And while you are in that mode, be open to what you need to do as well to grow. This includes modeling the great leaders you look up to or who helped you along in your own career. Is there something those leaders say or do that you feel, by adopting it, would make you an even better leader?

Stay open to learning what those attributes, traits, and even methods are and then giving them a try. Don't let your ego get in the way of you truly being the best leader you can be and the one you want to be.

Build an Atmosphere of Safety

I've mentioned this before, but it bears repeating here: Part of a team's growth is in learning to share ideas, and part of your growth as their leader is in making it feel safe for them to do that. Make sure that the team finds their working environment a safe one for ideas and feedback — that it encourages a growth and learning mindset for the whole team.

> Part of a team's growth is in learning to share ideas, and part of your growth as their leader is in making it feel safe for them to do that.

I'll take that a step further and say to make it a place that out-right encourages people to participate in the free flow of thought. No one should ever feel they should keep an idea to themselves out of fear that someone will make fun of it or dismiss it.

Remember, they're the ones doing their job, and they have a perspective you likely don't.

I've found that some of the best ideas come from a start-ing idea that was tweaked a little. The original idea started the whole shebang, and the person who came up with it will take great pride in being the one who sparked it. You should recog-nize them, too.

I have yet to find a team that isn't chock-full of ideas, but that doesn't mean their leader knows it. Their thoughts may have been squashed at some point or another, by someone else along the way, and maybe they're afraid to voice those thoughts now.

Ask them for all their ideas. Even if the concepts need a little polishing, really take in what they're sharing with you, think it through, and make sure they see you writing down the ideas. Then? Well then, come back to the team about them after a while.

Let them see that you considered their idea, even if you didn't do it exactly as they suggested — if not, explain why. They need to know those things too. They'll grow in leaps and bounds from thinking, problem-solving, and sharing. Celebrate all of those moments, and you'll see more of them — guaranteed.

Notice

Notice what skills and abilities your team members have or don't have. What do they excel at? What do they need to work on? Tell them. Let them know you see and appreciate what they're good at, and when they need improvement, show them that you're in their corner and that you know what they are capable of.

And don't forget to also notice what they've accomplished — even the smallest of things. Praise them in public, which lets recognition become a celebration for the whole team — do that whenever you can and when appropriate.

On the flip side, always correct your team members in private. Never, as in never *ever*, correct them in front of others. The humiliation of receiving criticism in front of peers or clients can send trust, belief, confidence, and any admiration of you speeding in the wrong direction.

If They're Struggling with Change

Some people view change as a judgment of sorts, and this can happen with employees too. Asking them to change, in their minds, can feel as though you're saying everything they've accomplished up to now is wrong. They may feel like you're brushing aside their efforts — which they were likely once proud of — as worthless. Like you're dismissing their hard work to this point. They may even decide they won't dare trust that feeling of accomplishment again because someone else may come along and shoot that down too.

Their reaction in this situation is often displayed as anger, or rebellion in the form of checking out or shutting down or, worse, simply refusing to change. But underneath all of that, they could be afraid that they're a failure. They may feel that they're unable to learn anything new and fear even more that you may tell them that. For some, they'd rather fear that than ever hear it said out loud.

If this is the case with anyone on your team, you'll need to help them through it and pay attention to what they need along the way. They may need a little more help understanding that, with growth, they'll gain something and take a step forward. Then when they are ready, they'll learn more because of it. All the steps are still there and important; in fact, they're the necessary foundation for everything to come.

Teach them that learning one thing never goes away just because the next new thing is absorbed. Rather, it's more like a stacking of new skills one on top of the other; nothing gets replaced or thrown away. It means there are now new things to add to what they already know and can do.

Dealing with Emotional Baggage

Oftentimes people who have experienced a difficult childhood have a tough time learning. Because of their experience, they may have had to rely heavily on their survival skills early on, which they had to develop themselves. Growing, changing, and taking new steps can feel as though they will be abandoning the only thing that carried them through. It's all they know. After all, they made it this far with those skills. Why try anything new? Scary stuff for someone in this situation.

If this is the case, you must build the person's trust by being consistent and encouraging them to take baby steps into new territory. Then, be there to answer questions, be on the sidelines, and recognize the improvement when they need that.

Remember, this could be very new territory for them, and they may never have had someone rooting for or guiding them. It can make for slow going, but it can totally be worth it.

Ultimately, with your encouragement, they will begin to see that those very survival skills are still there. They're just being used in a new way. They'll see that those skills come in handy, helping to make it easier to learn and take on new challenges. In fact, once an employee in this type of situation sees that they can conquer change, I've found they generally excel rapidly. After all, they learned early on to make things happen, and they naturally apply this ability to their work when they feel safe to take a few steps forward.

IT'S A CHOICE

I wish I had some actual magic to share with you to make this easier — maybe a formula you could put in a spreadsheet to graph the answers to the "be a great leader" equation. Or perhaps a supplement to take, and voilà, your team is happy, growing, and developing on their own. But I don't.

It's just not possible to get it in a pill because the magic of that growth only comes from the work of going through it. You've just got to *want* to be the kind of leader who loves people and loves supporting them as they move along in their careers.

I think most leaders are like that on some level. I also think that most of the rest just haven't felt it yet. Once you do, however, it's a greater sense of fulfillment than anything you could ever do yourself.

Leading requires that you shift the pride away from who you are and what you've accomplished to what your team achieves. Oh, you'll get some of that pride back, mind you, but it comes in the form of true gratitude for having shared this time with them as they discovered what they could do. And the knowledge that you were there — that you helped.

> **Leading requires that you shift the pride away from who you are and what you've accomplished to what your team achieves.**

That's because leading in this way combines the powerful feelings of accomplishment *and* those you get from giving. Both are fulfilling and I promise you, you'll want more.

See?

Now that's *your* growth.

#12

HOW YOU TREAT (AND TEACH) YOUR EMPLOYEES = HOW YOUR CUSTOMERS ARE TREATED

It carries forward.

Ever been to a store or fast-food drive-through and you find that you're saying to yourself, "Does *anyone* care about customer service anymore?" Or how about when you're at the counter and the four employees on the other side of it are chatting each other up about last night's party instead of waiting on the customers (and they don't dare make any eye contact)?

Does this bug you?

It bugs me. A lot, actually. In a situation like this, I have to admit, I no longer care how good the product is. The service just makes it suck, anyway.

But you've got to wonder. Why? Why don't these employees care? What's going on here?

You guessed it: It all comes back to leadership.

SERVICE: THE GOOD, THE BAD, AND YOU

Service, good or bad, sticks with a customer and is remembered and shared for years to come. You owe it to your customers to remember this. Don't believe me? Here are two examples.

Plumb Tuckered Out

I have a friend who recently shared a story with me. She had called a local plumbing company to repair an issue in her home. The plumber did the work amiably enough, and she soon found he was the talkative type. He confided in her that he was tired because he'd been working a lot of overtime that week as his boss typically demanded. He explained that he was never given much time off by his employer. The extra hours resulted in him not having any time to spend with his family.

After he left, my friend discovered that the plumber hadn't quite completed the repair, and she had to call the company back. They sent the same plumber back out. He apologized, explaining he was probably so tired from the long work hours that he had overlooked something.

True or not, the plumber was openly sharing his negative opinion of his employer directly with the customer. Whether my friend believed or agreed with the gentleman, the earful she got left a dubious impression of the company he worked for, how they treated their employees, and the service it had resulted in. She thought twice before calling them again.

Employees who feel they are unfairly treated are usually miserable at work, which makes for a terrible spirit and energy. That is the same energy they bring to and share with your customers. They may not even intend to harm the customer relationship; it's just an outlet for sharing their feelings when they don't feel safe to do so with their leader.

As a leader, you have to pay attention to how your team is feeling. If something needs to be fixed, you fix it.

This Icy Reception Worked

A few years ago, I attended a yoga conference that was quite strenuous, with long days of practice. I had a knee in bad shape at that point but was managing to limp (literally) through the days.

Following one particularly difficult day, I hobbled into my hotel lobby with my angry knee screaming at me to stop moving immediately. The gentleman at the front desk noticed my grimace and limp and asked whether I was okay. I managed a tiny smile and mumbled something about I'd be fine by morning, thanked him, and went on to my room.

About 15 minutes later, there was a knock at my door. Walking even one foot was misery, but I stumbled over to open it. To my surprise, the young man from the front desk stood there with two freezer-size ziplock bags full of ice. He said he had noticed I was having trouble walking and thought the ice bags would help.

He was right.

That ice helped a lot, and the thoughtfulness he showed helped a lot too. The level of service I received that day told me a great deal about how this gentleman felt about his job and how he'd been trained to take care of his guests. He was truly there to take care of me.

I don't remember the young man's name, but I never forgot his kindness. And I never will.

By the way, I try to always make it a point to stay in that same hotel chain every time I travel.

I ♥ you, Marriott.

WHAT YOU DO GOES FURTHER THAN YOU THINK

A wonderful thing happens when you feel as though someone wants to take care of you. Those words even strike some feels as I write them — "take care of you."

Not to get too mushy or anything, okay maybe a little, but I think we're designed to be caring and giving; divinely wired, as I mentioned before. Has there ever been a time in your life when you did something charitable or kind and said to yourself afterward, "Well, *that* was stupid; never doing *that* again!"

I'll go out on a limb here and say the answer is, probably not. In fact, you most likely felt just the opposite.

We get a great feeling when we help and give to others, like it's the right thing to do.

When asked this question, my leadership development program participants have never said they felt anything other than great after they've helped someone. Service brings this same feeling of giving. And I think we were designed to feel that way on purpose.

Why?

Because, as I discussed earlier in the book, *every* company is a service provider. No matter what you make or do for your customers, it's a service. And it's a service that helps them in some way.

When you have this attitude about service and deal with your employees in this way, you will teach the same mindset to them and reinforce its importance. And if I'm right, that giving, helping, which includes providing great service, feels good — imagine how that feels to your team when they catch on to that.

Cool, right?

The truth is that how you treat your employees is pretty much *exactly* how they interact with your customers. So how you teach them about service is important.

I like to call this "leadership math." But this isn't a simple $1 + 1 = 2$. It's more like $1 + 1 = \infty$.

One of my favorite quotes on this subject is attributed to Jeff Weiner, former CEO of LinkedIn, who said, "Inspire, empower, listen, and appreciate. Practicing any one of these can improve employee engagement; mastering all four can change the game."[29]

This mentality is clearly a fuel behind his success at LinkedIn. He is noted for always having an eye on the future while maintaining a leadership style that emphasizes empathy, which he promoted in the company's culture.

"Under his guidance, LinkedIn has nurtured a culture where employees feel valued and understood," wrote Tejas Tahmankar in *Mirror Review Blog*, adding that the culture is seen as a strategic advantage by many.

They're basing that on the fact that through it, LinkedIn grew its user base by 1945.45 percent, with a revenue surge of 10094.87 percent, during his 11 years there.[30] And I promise I didn't add any extra numbers in those statistics; this is really what happened.

Looks like he treated his employees well, all right, and they indeed treated and serviced the customers well, too. There's an example of what great leaders can do by focusing on their teams. More on that later — much more.

Back to service, though. When I'm in the type of situation where service doesn't seem to be on the menu, I immediately think to myself, *Those employees must not be treated very well*, or, *They haven't trained them at all*.

A bit "judgy" of me, but I'll just bet you've had the same thoughts a time or two. It's the opposite with good service — it can make even an average product seem better. And sometimes, as my Marriott story shows, it can go much further and make a huge difference.

CAN YOU SAY, CORE VALUE?

Your team will know by the emphasis you place on service, and on teaching them about it, that it's important. This includes you providing great service to them as their leader.

If great service is what you want your team and company to be known for, make it a part of who you are as a company. And make it a part of who you are as a leader.

Make it a core value.

Now, I know people will sometimes start rolling their eyes when they hear "core values," and honestly, your team may be among them. I've found that this is usually because core values are so often said, put in print, written on web-

This includes you providing great service to them as their leader.

sites, etc. that they become invisible in a way. They're said but not made important.

Maybe it's the way they're presented, or how genuine or stuffy they sound, how short or long they are, or how those up the management chain live and lead by them (or don't).

Probably all of that.

But core values are no joke, especially if providing the best service possible is one of them. They are a great rock to stand on and should be a declaration of what the company and you both stand for. And they should be a reminder of what everyone in the organization is expected to align with.

Core values must also be reflected in your policies if they are to be taken seriously. But your team would say, "You go first."

And they're right.

If you don't align with the values of your company but let your team know they are expected to, your message is diluted by your actions. And, for that matter, you run the risk of diluting all policies in some way as well.

Establishing a solid service mindset does indeed require some work, and you have to do the work more than just once. It's like that gas tank of your car mentioned earlier in the book; you've just gotta fill it back up now and then.

Bringing the importance of service back to the forefront in your company from time to time is a great reminder for everyone there. It can be a core value, verbally stated, a tagline with your logo, a motto, or even something on the walls of your company.

But have it somewhere and come back to it often. Make it a part of what you do every day and in every interaction. Make it expected.

And you, as their leader, have to apply it to how you lead your team every day. You are a service provider as well in this way — never forget that.

Let's go a step further, why don't we?

It's About Each Other Too

Make the value of great service also part of how your team treats each other. While they're learning to be great service providers, they also need to learn that it's part of how they are together. We covered cliques earlier, and it's worth briefly mentioning them again here. If employees treat each other badly, as most cliques are known to do, this isn't a good example of service.

Light bulb moment, right? Your team may not think of themselves as service providers to each other, but they are. Teach them that, and then make it expected in their role.

Think about that for a moment. They're seeing and hearing a core value about service. They're seeing you model it. And now they know they are expected to provide it to each other, as well as to their customers.

Gotta love consistency.

If your team sees that you will not let the value of service fade away, that you expect it at every level, they'll adjust to keeping it in mind too.

YOU'RE ALL IN IT TOGETHER

Teach your team that no matter their role, ultimately, they all funnel into taking care of each other and the customer. Whatever part they play — whether it's buying widget parts, making widgets, dreaming up new widgets, or telling the customer about them — it all boils down to taking care of the customer because they want or need some of those widgets.

For every interaction — from how your team is led, to how they engage with each other, to how they communicate with the customer — the experience of the interaction matters just as much as the products.

And *everyone's* role in getting that product to the customer plays a part in that moment when it arrives at their door.

> *Everyone's* role in getting that product to the customer plays a part in that moment when it arrives at their door.

#13

HOW GREAT A LEADER YOU ARE IS UP TO YOU

Read that again.

I say this with love, and yes, a little bit in your face.

Just a little.

But it's only because I want you to be the leader you *want* to be, and I believe this is an important part of it.

It's *all* up to you. Your circumstances don't matter. Your choices do.

There's just no room for even the tiniest bit of victim mentality in a great leader. In fact, it will hold you

> There's just no room for even the tiniest bit of victim mentality in a great leader.

and your team back as you work to develop the next generation of leaders too.

How great a leader you are is squarely, and fully, on your shoulders right now, and it starts as simply as making the decision (also right now) about what type you want to be. And it's a simple decision when you come right down to it. It's one you may have to make more than once, but I encourage you to make it, and so does your team.

It doesn't matter where you came from, what challenges you had or have, what school you went to, how much money you had or have (or don't have), or what store you bought your clothes at.

What may or may not have happened to you doesn't excuse you from making the decision to be a great leader, and it never gives you a go-pass not to try.

Focusing on what went wrong in life has never inspired anyone to be greater, reach farther, or achieve more. The same is true for you. Being a great leader comes from simply deciding to do what you can do now and then going forward with it, or deciding what you need to let go of or move out of your way and then doing that.

These decisions and actions, not your situation, make you the leader you want to be.

THE HIDDEN CHALLENGES OF JOHN IRVING

History is full of examples of great leaders and great minds who faced enormous challenges and disabilities but didn't let any of these stop them. One who comes to mind is author John

Irving, one of the most celebrated American writers in history. Irving has written 19 books, his first one at age 26, including memoirs. His novels include classics such as *The World According to Garp* and *The Cider House Rules*.

He has received numerous awards for his writing, including a National Book Award and an Academy Award for the screenplay adaptation of *The Cider House Rules*.

No one would argue Irving's genius and gift, yet he has managed all of this while struggling with dyslexia.

You might think that someone who has dyslexia — a learning disorder directly affecting reading and spelling — might be too challenged by a writing career, in particular. And he didn't have it easy early on. He was even labeled as "stupid" by many of his teachers while he was growing up and was put in a remedial spelling class after he failed English.[31]

But rather than focusing on how the disorder made things harder for him, Irving saw his dyslexia as a plus. "It's become an advantage," he's quoted as saying. "In writing a novel, it doesn't hurt anybody to have to go slowly."

His learning disability may have made him slow down, but that also made him pay twice as much attention to what he was writing, and he felt that going slowly made him improve it along the way.

Irving is clearly gifted, and his dyslexia may well have fueled his writing genius. At least he seems to see it that way by all accounts.

All I know is that I, along with a whole lot of other folks throughout the world, love his works — all 19 of them.

I also hope he keeps the books coming for years to come, as well as the inspiration his story provides to us all.

BE THE EXAMPLE

With all he faced, Mr. Irving could have just remained stuck in thoughts about his challenges with dyslexia. He could have just decided it was impossible to do anything, let alone become an author, and let that decision guide his life. Had he done that, his life would likely have gone in a very different direction.

But, thank goodness, he chose not to.

His circumstances didn't define or limit him one iota. Instead, Irving chose to see them as a part of his life and the fuel to make his writing even better. And what a path it's been for him.

Your circumstances shouldn't define you, either. They're not an example of what you are or an excuse for what you can't accomplish, and that includes being the best leader you can be.

You don't have to get stuck in your circumstances; you can use them to propel you forward. As Irving did, you can choose to see the unique perspective they may have gifted you with as an advantage for doing something in a new and different way in the world. Becoming an example like Irving doesn't happen through the spoken word. It comes from doing, and from showing how to stay focused on what *could* be, rather than what *is or was.*

Your team watches for those examples because they have their own challenges to navigate. They take from your example how to make any circumstance positive because you show them not only that it actually *is* possible but also how to do it.

What you've overcome will encourage your people to overcome their own problems and reach for something more, and fill them up with dreams to do big things all along the way.

They'll see it's possible through your example of having done it.

Your unique challenges in life are not necessarily part of their purpose and inspiration to come in to work each day, but your example of how to keep going when the going is rough 100 percent is.

HOW YOU SHARE YOUR STORY IS ALSO AN EXAMPLE

When your team knows your story, it can inspire them, but only if handled well. You'll want to watch out that you aren't focusing on the wrong thing.

This makes me think of a colleague I once had. Their every story ended with a statement of how someone else had told them how wonderful they were. No matter where the story started or what it was about, you could bet your paycheck that it was going to end with someone having proclaimed them the nicest, sweetest, or most-est something or other they'd ever known.

After a while, I just knew (we all did) to sit there and wait for the punch line of their greatness so that I would know the story was coming to an end. I'm not proud of that, but that's what would happen. And sure enough, the greatness line would come, and then we could move on with the meeting or discussion.

Are you guilty of this? I've done it a time or two and I'm not proud of it.

Step out of the limelight and put your team in it. That's where they should be. Remember — you're cheering them on, not the other way around. Focus on them, supporting their growth and celebrating achievements along the way. Help them stretch and take on more of the things they want to do, and help them get the training they need to do that. And give them the inspiration to try.

They'll love you for that forever and never forget it.

Three Tips for Not Being the "Punch Line" Person

None of us wants to be that Punch Line Guy (or Gal), or anything like him. Here are some ways to make sure you don't get into that mode without realizing it.

Avoid becoming the victim in the story. We've already talked about this, but it's sometimes a lot easier to say than do. However, your story is not something your team needs to understand from the perspective of a victim. The focus needs to be on the fact that a challenge can be overcome, not on how much sympathy you deserve. You're not asking for any hall passes, remember? You don't get to with this, either.

Avoid becoming the main focus. Take care to sprinkle into conversations what *you've* overcome or done in very small portions, and only when needed. Otherwise, it will get in the way of what *they* are dreaming of and will shift the focus to you. Your shared experience is meant to reassure and inspire, not to make you the center of attention.

Humility is a beautiful thing, and it's one of the best tools of leadership. Bring it into each day and apply it generously.

> Humility is a beautiful thing, and it's one of the best tools of leadership. Bring it into each day and apply it generously.

Avoid hero mentality too. Those who faced challenges in their lives sometimes go to an extreme to overcome them, even perhaps seeking to prove their value by aiming for being perfect — aka, being the hero.

Let's be honest, underneath it all, hero mentality is just another form of victim mentality in most cases. It's a person's way of coping with the impact of the challenges they had by trying to be the absolute best of all time, at all they do — as in better than anyone ever — and to be that for everyone who crosses their path.

It's also a complete no-win situation, especially for leaders. Why?

First of all, there's no way to overcome something in the past by struggling to be perfect, including being the perfect rescuer for others. That in itself is a cycle of struggle, disappointment, and exhaustion; and that keeps going round and round, fueled by self-doubt.

Like perfectionism, the hero mentality is fleeting; it's an illusion. You're human, after all, and you *will* mess up at some point.

Second, there's your team and the impact your drive for heroics can have on them. Even though you might actually *be* the hero in some way in your team's eyes as their leader (and probably are), it's not a conclusion you should try to encourage your team to draw, intentionally or not.

That can put the focus on you, rather than on your team where it belongs.

Besides, if you're aiming for being perfect or garnering a hero title, your team will think you expect that of them too. Remember, perfectionism isn't possible, and it's setting them up for misery and failure. It's not inspiring, it's not good leadership, and they will leave and go somewhere else that doesn't make them feel that they can't cut it.

Here's something to remember: Nobody is perfect. Including you. But your team will still love you anyway.

Actually, they'll love you all the more when you show them you flub, too, but then you humbly get right back up and in the saddle.

That's as perfect as it gets.

ARE YOU IN YOUR OWN WAY?

Leading authentically can reveal a lot about us *to* ourselves. Insecurities, bad habits, bad experiences that linger, or just lack of understanding — these can all get in the way. It's worth the effort to figure them out. I want you to be the best leader you have decided to be, regardless of the challenges you may have faced or are facing now.

I mentioned that, often, hero mode and perfectionism go together. Best to examine those obstacles and any others that are blocking you — because they can and do block your team from the happiness they'll get from working authentically as well.

So, if there's one question I recommend you ask yourself to help with this challenge, it's this one:

What's really in my way of being a better leader? Is it that I'm trying to be a hero? Trying to be perfect?

If you are, then the next question is: *Why?*

You might need to ask why several times after that to question those reasons, too, because each answer may peel back another layer until you hear and feel the real answer reveal itself. But it's there.

Find out what the stumbling block is, and then change it. Be brave, ask the questions, and do the work. Go on now, you've got this.

But Wait — There's More

There's another question that depends on the one we just discussed. This one goes like this:

What type of company and team do I want to have in five years? Heck, what about one or two years? Tomorrow?

That all depends on the leader you decide to be today.

As in right now.

If you want to do better, do it. If you want to be a better leader, do that too.

Do it today. Right now.

If you want to have a team that is thriving and growing to be among your next round of great leaders, add that to the list.

Not much happens in work and life without a plan, and this is no exception. Deciding what type of company you want to have down the line includes being the type of leader who gets and keeps you there.

Scary? A little. This is not just hard work, it's heart work.

Worth it? A lot. Heart work is the new cool.

Go for it.

#14

IF YOU WANT PEOPLE TO WORK WITH THEIR HEARTS, YOU HAVE TO LEAD WITH YOURS

Every day. Even the bad days.

Leading from the heart is a 24-7 kind of thing. Whether the day is rough or great shouldn't matter. Is it always easy to do, especially when the poop might be hitting the fan?

Nope.

It's just always worth it.

So, keep that Leadership Golden Rule we talked about before in mind, because as with that, leading with heart should *always* apply. It may look a little different from one day to the next, but your leadership should always come from that place that makes you what you are — human. That makes it personal, just as it should be.

That's the same place you want your team to work from each day — their hearts.

News flash — they want to work that way too, with purpose.

The heart is where they are engaged, purposeful, committed, and part of what they're doing for you and how they are serving others while doing it. But they will always look to you for the example and motivation to come back to that place of heart in their work.

You are the example. And if your team members see you doing it, good times and bad, they will seek to do the same. That goes for their jobs now and the leadership roles they may have in the future — and to the future leaders they may develop as well.

THEY WILL REMEMBER

One of my favorite quotes is one often attributed to Maya Angelou: "They may forget what you said, but they will never forget how you made them feel." I often reference this quote as one of my favorite thoughts on leadership when I'm speaking. It's so popular that, without fail, nearly everyone in the audience can speak the last line out loud for me when I ask them to.

I think it sums up what is true about people. That what they remember most about interacting with someone and what sticks are the emotions they're left with. They may even forget the subject of the conversation, but good or bad, they'll remember the feeling.

It's one of the best pieces of leadership advice I know of.

Turns out, however, Angelou was not the first to use this sentiment. It had always been my perception that she had, and I think that's what most people believe too.

But, while she is quoted as saying something very similar, the concept in the quote was actually first attributed in 1971 to Carl Buehner, a one-time general authority of the Church of Jesus Christ of Latter-day Saints.[32]

It's easy to think Angelou was the first. After all, she seemed to live her life inspiring many people with her words and wisdom, encouraging us to be better humans.

She was brilliant and is one of the people I have always most admired in my life. I love her work, as millions of people do.

I think what matters most is that two influential people who were admired and respected in their fields both said essentially the same thing. What's most important is how people feel after interacting with you.

That's what people remember, always.

A DADDYISM TO LEARN FROM

My dad faced just about every disadvantage you can imagine growing up, but somehow managed to come through it all and become a successful businessman along the way. I looked up to him more than anyone I ever have or will. I admired his sheer will and perseverance through the toughest of times and hope that in some way I have honored him for it.

He had a lot of successes in his life, and some failures too. But he always tried to live with integrity and honor. We had a fiery father-daughter relationship when I was young, but we found our way through that, and I am forever grateful for the closeness I had with him in the end.

Funny what you can work through when love is the foundation.

Years ago, I wrote a paper on "Daddyisms" to honor all that my father had taught me growing up. One in particular comes to mind when I'm thinking about leadership.

> **Funny what you can work through when love is the foundation.**

I was suffering from a broken heart at that time. My father wasn't a man of many words, or the gushy, huggy type of dad either. But he spoke directly from the heart when he did speak, and I remember this moment clearly.

I had just gone through a rough breakup with someone and was trying (not very successfully) to keep it together. During a family gathering, he came over and stood very close, shoulder to shoulder. He leaned in and whispered quietly into my ear, "Don't let them make you cold."

He was referring to people, of course. Those who are in your life or will be in some form or fashion and who will hurt you in some way. I think he was referring to life too, and not to ever let it or others take from me what God has given all of us — the ability to love and care for people.

I think this also applies to leaders.

If, as a leader, all you do is think about the bottom line, the assets and liabilities, the processes, etc., that's where your energy goes. Even though those things are important in a company, there's no emotional return from them. That only comes from the other humans you interact with — your team, your own teammates, and even your customers.

Without that emotional exchange, things can get chilly over time. We can start to disconnect from each other. During my career, I've seen this happen to folks. People lose some piece of their humanity at work, but they keep seeking it, and in the wrong direction. It's a terrible cycle, and ultimately, they can become unhappy and might start to burn out and shut down.

We leaders are humans too. We need to know the numbers and the competition and such, but we also need to keep our hearts in the game for our teams. If we forget that, either they will move on to someplace where they feel the heart from their leadership, or they will take the cold, disconnected example as a way of being for themselves. We don't want that, and neither do they.

IT'S NOT ALWAYS EASY

The problem with working with heart is that, as in your personal life, your heart will probably get broken at times. Your team may even be the one breaking it. As much as I hate writing it, they may do things such as lie about you or betray you.

This is one of the toughest parts of leadership. Particularly if you're trying hard to help them, and then they seem to turn against you.

So what?

Before you get too mad at me for saying that, hear me out. I don't say it lightly; in fact, I know all too well how it feels to be betrayed. Teams can forget that *you* are human too.

I'll say it again. So what?

Remember: They're growing and developing. But even more important, this is what you decided to be — their leader. The type of leader you have decided to be is not based on someone else or their behaviors.

As we talked about earlier, who you are, and the leader you've decided to be, is up to you.

When your heart is broken, remember first that it doesn't happen every day. But it is likely to happen at some point in your career as a leader. When it does happen, it stings, just as you would expect it might. It's not an easy part of leadership, as I said earlier, but it's one you need to prepare for. You see, your team is likely still growing and learning. That's why you're there — to help them with that, and that includes how they treat people at work, including you.

When they do let you down, come back first to your responsibility. You're the leader, the teacher, the one helping them grow. Unless it was something unforgivable, it's best to view the incident as a teaching and leading moment. And, provided it's not unforgiveable, a circumstance where they've hurt you is a great opportunity to teach by example. You can show the team what's wrong about their behavior and why. You will show them how to handle adversity and conflict, how to forgive as a human, and how to carry on as a leader.

Your team will learn more from watching you walk that walk than from just about any other situation. And one day, they'll thank you for it by making the same decision — to stay focused on moving forward and helping their own team to grow in the process.

Now that's a cycle that works.

IT'S NOT CALLED "MANAGERSHIP"

There's a difference between managing and leading. After all, we refer to the word "leadership," not "managership." Managing by definition, according to Merriam-Webster, is "to exercise executive, administrative, and supervisory direction of." Managing is important — it's taking care of the processes, the procedures, making sure that all the widget parts are where they need to be, when they need to be there, and that the teams who need them know how to use them.

But leadership has a slightly different definition. It's pulling a team together, enabling them and inspiring them to do something. It's having the vision of where things are headed and the strategy to get there, as well as inspiring everyone to see the plan and know their part.

One way to look at it is as if you have a ship — an actual ship. In this scenario, a manager is busy overseeing the rowing and making sure everyone has the right oar and has been properly trained in its use. The manager is very involved in the operations of the initiative, the process, the procedures, and such, all of which is incredibly important. If there's no wind, someone has to row, and the more efficient the rowers, the faster they'll move the ship through the water.

But the leader, she's up on the bridge plotting the course for the ship and everyone there. She's making sure she has communicated her vision for the journey they're about to go on together and has let the others know their role in it and why it's important. She makes sure they feel good about it. This includes the managers as well, because the leader is responsible for them too.

They're both important, the managers and the leaders, and they're in the same boat, along with the team. What makes them similar is that they care about the people and each other, and they understand the importance of the journey.

What makes them *different* is their focus — the manager focusing on the operations and processes; the leader, on the vision and journey. Both are important and both play a part in getting everyone "on board," so to speak, and in arriving together.

WHAT MAKES A GREAT LEADER?

We talked about jerks and jerk-y behavior already, about losing our poop and looking funny when we do. We also covered the problems with FIFB and cliques.

(Get rid of them.)

But I think we need to talk about the attributes that make a leader great. Just as with jerk-y behaviors, when I ask, "What qualities make a great leader?" during a presentation, the audience is equally quick with their answers, which typically include:

- Kind
- Caring
- Thoughtful
- Honest
- Has integrity
- Mentor
- Coach
- Bold
- Innovative

Just as with the bad behaviors of leaders, none of these good behaviors is produced by business acumen or software. There's also no mention of golfing, Ping-Pong™ tables, or free crackers in the break room — all of these things are fun, but they don't show up in the answers I hear from groups.

Just hasn't happened. Why do you think that's true?

Well, what do you notice about the points above? They all have something in common.

They're all personal.

What would you add to the list?

Which do you bring in each day and lead your team with? Which do you need to bring in more?

These are great questions to ask yourself, and really great questions to answer.

GREAT LEADERSHIP IS AN ACT OF LOVE

It is. Leadership is a form of service to others, and I also believe that a sense of service comes from that place in us that loves other people.

But, hey, as Steve Farber would say, if the word "love" bugs you in relation to the workplace, call it something else. Maybe "honesty" would work, or even "caring," "being considerate," "humble," and so on. I assure you, however, regardless of the word you choose, if love is the intention, people feel cared for (and, yes, loved) when they are provided with great leadership. This is true of your customers through your act of providing them great service, and certainly true of your team through how they are led.

If you focus only on the business and the bottom line, the team won't be engaged to grow.

Focus on growing them, and they will naturally pour into their work what they have to give. Then the business benefits.

You're building something special, so you need a next generation of great leaders to keep it going. Just love 'em (or whatever you want to call it), and forgive them when you need to.

Show your team a better way of being a leader so that they learn to bring that to work for themselves. And they learn to do the things that help them always want to learn more. Pour into them so much that they pour even more into their work to create something remarkable and then grow into the leaders they have the potential to be. They'll be paying forward what you've taught them and shaping the future of leadership in their own ways and through those new leaders who they have the pleasure of teaching.

There's a quote I once read by author Betty Bender that speaks to this issue of working with your heart and encouraging your team to do the same: "When people go to work, they shouldn't have to leave their hearts at home."

Exactly.

THANK YOU, DERRICK

That Derrick was something, all right.

I bet he had no idea what he started in me all those years ago with his story, and even less of an idea where it would lead. He certainly didn't have a clue I would one day write a book about it.

That makes two of us.

Just goes to show you how inspiration works.

Him telling me that story changed me forever. I can't say I always did my best as a leader at everything, by the way — I am certainly far from perfect. However, his story sparked an interest in me to pay attention to what teams want and how they feel about how they're led, including my own needs as I navigated my own career. I became very curious about how to create a better workplace for everyone, leaders and teams alike.

Turns out it's not that hard.

Just be human.

Realizing this changed my own approach to leadership. Though I've not been perfect at leading, I feel I have been far better than I would have been without Derrick's story launching me on a lifetime quest of paying attention to people at work.

It also changed how I interact and communicate in my personal life. I tend to want to push through and get things done. That check mark makes me feel some kind of fantastic. But I learned through the years that sometimes, someone else may need to ponder a thing a bit longer.

Turns out, I need those people. I need the ponderers on my team just as much as the ones who like to jump quickly.

As leaders, we must learn when each type of person is needed and what they need from us — and, most important, we must realize we need them all.

Derrick's story was an eye- and heart-opener that showed me how people feel at work and how they feel about leadership. Knowing how it affected him affected me. I've remained on the lookout for "Derricks" in the world as my career has progressed, and I've been one myself a time or two.

> As leaders, we must learn when each type of person is needed and what they need from us — and, most important, we must realize we need them all.

Those times were some of the best lessons, and I'm grateful to be able to look back on them now and then.

So, coming full circle to him, his story, and its impact seems like the right thing to do.

Thank you, Derrick.

I never forgot you, and I never will.

And also, I need to thank all the teams I've worked with, the leaders I've had, and the ones I've had the great honor of leading in my career thus far.

It's been quite the trip.

I've loved every minute of it almost as much as I've loved all of you. I hope in some way my own lessons have made you consider a few things that could help you become an even better leader.

If so, I encourage you to lean into those things and watch how they change you.

Then watch how your team changes too.

Pay attention to what you need and pay attention to what they need. Then pay attention to how it all comes together to make for a better workplace and team who enjoy driving to work on Monday morning and feeling their purpose each day in the service of others.

So go on now, love your team in your own way, whether that be by calling it caring or calling it honesty — or use your own word.

They all work.

Help your team achieve all the things they want to. Believe me, there is no downside to that, and never any regret. Not even a little.

It's simply the right thing to do.

And that is so very *personal*, from me to you.

ENDNOTES

1   *Jaws*, directed by Steven Spielberg (Universal Pictures, 1975).

2   Duncan Coombe, "Don't Take It Personally
    Is Terrible Work Advice," *Harvard Business
    Review*, March 29, 2016, https://hbr.org/2016/03/
    dont-take-it-personally-is-terrible-work-advice.

3   T.A. Group Holdings, "Not Personal, Just Business,"
    June 15, 2023, https://tagroupholdings.com/2023/06/15/
    not-personal-just-business/.

4   Great Place to Work, "Three Predictions for the
    Workplace Culture of the Future."

5   Ted Kitterman, "When Employees Thrive, Companies
    More Than Triple Their Stock Market Performance,"
    Great Place to Work, April 16, 2024, https://www.great-
    placetowork.com/resources/blog/when-employees-thrive-
    companies-triple-their-stock-market-performance.

6   Ted Kitterman, "When Employees Thrive, Companies
    More Than Triple Their Stock Market Performance,"
    Great Place to Work, April 16, 2024, https://www.great-
    placetowork.com/resources/blog/when-employees-thrive-
    companies-triple-their-stock-market-performance.

7   Society for Human Resource Management, "Essential
    Elements of Employee Retention," *SHRM Blog*,
    October 17, 2017, https://lrshrm.shrm.org/blog/2017/10/
    essential-elements-employee-retention.

8   Indeed Editorial Team, "How to Build a Business Culture
    in 2023," *Indeed*, accessed September 19, 2024, https://www.
    indeed.com/hire/c/info/business-in-culture?gad_source=1&gcl

id=CjwKCAjwnqK1BhBvEiwAi7o0XyAhmopsb6RZvUbrdQx
kSJqSBlIa0DW5rfm3ZK_YIvxVXQuebR5BQxoCNg4QAvD_
BwE&gbraid=0AAAAADfh6_ssqJY07ba2e9aUCLpEZ-
np8&aceid=&gclsrc=aw.ds.

9   Darren Dahl, "Who Says Business Isn't Personal?" *The Great Game of Business Blog*, June 2, 2020, https://www.greatgame.com/blog/who-says-business-isnt-personal.

10 Socialigence, "A Brief History of Emotional Intelligence," accessed October 11, 2024, https://www.socialigence.net/blog/a-brief-history-of-emotional-intelligence/.

11 Daniel Goleman, *Emotional Intelligence: Why It Can Matter More Than IQ*, Kindle edition, p. vi (Random House Publishing Group, 2020).

12 CareerBuilder. "Forty-Three Percent of Workers Say Their Office Has Cliques, Finds CareerBuilder Survey," *PR Newswire*, last modified July 18, 2013, accessed September 19, 2024, https://www.prnewswire.com/news-releases/forty-three-percent-of-workers-say-their-office-has-cliques-finds-careerbuilder-survey-216710851.

13 "Groupthink," *Psychology Today*, accessed January 7, 2025, https://www.psychologytoday.com/us/basics/groupthink.

14 Joshua A. Luna, "The Toxic Effects of Branding Your Workplace a 'Family,'" *Harvard Business Review*, October 27, 2021, https://hbr.org/2021/10/the-toxic-effects-of-branding-your-workplace-a-family.

15 Steve Farber, "Greater Than Yourself Keynote on Mentoring and Coaching," YouTube video, 4:22, January 7, 2010, https://www.youtube.com/watch?v=j2DkzOc8RwI.

16 The compilation is based on a similar one from Universal Enlightenment Forum, "8 Quotes on the Golden Rule from Across Religions," Medium, July 16, 2019, https://medium.

com/universal-enlightenment-forum/8-quotes-on-the-golden-rule-from-across-religions-bc4ac545b1c.

17 Matthew 7:12, New International Version, accessed January 18, 2025, https://www.biblegateway.com/passage/?search=Matthew%207&version=NIV.

18 Muhammad ibn Isma'il al-Bukhari, Sahih al-Bukhari, Book of Belief, Hadith 13, January 18, 2025, https://sunnah.com/bukhari:13.

19 The Complete Babylonian Talmud, Shabbat 31a, trans. Michael L. Rodkinson (Boston: The Talmud Society, 1918), 550, accessed January 18, 2025, https://archive.org/details/CompleteBabylonianTalmudEnglish.

20 Bahá'u'lláh, *Epistle to the Son of the Wolf*, pocket-size ed. (Wilmette, IL: US Bahá'í Publishing Trust, 1988), 181, accessed January 18, 2025, https://reference.bahai.org/en/t/b/ESW/esw-2.html.utf8?query=Choose%7Cthou%7Cthy%7Cneighbor%7Cthou%7Cchoosest%7Cthyself&action=highlight#pg30.

21 Mahabharata Online, "Mahabharata: Section 13, Chapter 78," accessed January 18, 2025, https://mahabharataonline.com/translation/mahabharata_13b078.php.

22 Dharmatrāta, Udanavarga, chap. 5, v. 18, trans. W. Woodville Rockhill (London: Trübner & Co., 1883).

23 Muslim: Moore, A. (2021), Muslim Family Life, "Extend the Kindness You Want," *Muslim Journal*, 46(20), 8.

24 Confucius, *The Analects of Confucius*, trans. James Legge (New York: Charles E. Tuttle Company, 1893), 15:24, https://archive.org/details/theanalectsconfucius/page/n501/mode/2up.

25 Jeffrey Wattles, "Plato's Brush with the Golden Rule," *The Journal of Religious Ethics*, 15(1), (1993), https://www.jstor.org/stable/40018144.

26 Thales of Miletus Quotes, Quoteikon, accessed October 12, 2024, https://www.quoteikon.com/thales-of-miletus-quotes.html.

27 Emanuel Cleaver, "Golden Rule," Congressman Emanuel Cleaver, accessed October 11, 2024, https://cleaver.house.gov/media-center/ec-dc/golden-rule#:~:text=The%20ancient%20Greek%20rhetorician%2C%20Isocrates,do%20not%20want%20done%20to.

28 Todd Coopee, "Weebles from Hasbro/Romper Room (1971)," Toy Tales, April 25, 2022, https://toytales.ca/weebles-from-hasbro-romper-room-1971/.

29 Jeff Weiner, "Inspire, empower, listen & appreciate. Practicing any one of these can improve employee engagement; mastering all four can change the game," LinkedIn, September 19, 2017, https://www.linkedin.com/posts/jeffweiner08_inspire-empower-listen-appreciatepracticing-activity-6316000113378496512-MkTU/.

30 Tejas Tahmankar, "5 Classic and Disruptive Jeff Weiner Leadership Styles," *Mirror Review Blog*, accessed November 15, 2024, https://blog.mirrorreview.com/jeff-weiner-leadership-styles/.

31 Dyslexia Help at the University of Michigan, "John Irving," *Dyslexia Help*, accessed November 16, 2024, https://dyslexiahelp.umich.edu/success-stories/john-irving.

32 Richard Evans, *Richard Evans' Quote Book* (Salt Lake City, Utah: Publishers Press, 1971), 244.

ABOUT THE AUTHOR

INDIE BOLLMAN is a respected leader in the corporate organizational development and human resources space, with more than 30 years' experience in leadership and executive roles. Her corporate experience has centered around companies in start-up or ramp-up modes, where she focused on building and developing teams and leaders, as well as addressing culture issues and transformations.

Always focused on current and innovative solutions, she is currently the owner of Indie Bollman Coaching and Consulting LLC, sharing her experience and passion for helping teams and businesses grow through public speaking, executive and leadership coaching, and training. In addition, she continues to work on books focused on leadership and improving organizational culture, and she has authored numerous articles, some featured on LinkedIn and others for the Society of Human Resources Management.

Indie was honored as one of the Pros to Know by *Supply & Demand Chain Executive* in 2023 for her contributions to organizational development in the transportation and logistics industry. She was also honored as a Woman of Influence in 2020 by the *Jacksonville Business Journal*.

A Florida native, Indie is an avid traveler who is forever curious about the world. Between travels, she enjoys coming home to her beloved sunshine state, where she resides with her family — including two cats, two dogs, and two Jeeps (can't forget those).

Contact

🌐 IndieBollman.com

✉️ Indie@IndieBollman.com

in IndiebBollman

📷 @IndieBollman

WANT MORE?

I've got you covered!

Go to my bonus content page on my website, where you can:

- Download **bonus Leadership Truth Bombs**
- Sign up for my **monthly newsletter with ideas, thoughts, and methods** to support you and your team
- Follow me on my social channels!

www.indiebollman.com/ltbbonus

GREAT LEADERS PUT PEOPLE FIRST

Leadership done right brings something to everyone —
your customers, your company, your people, and you. That
win-win approach is what brings growth and results.

The first step is creating your dream team to deliver on this
idea. Guess what? You probably already have a lot of the
right people. They just need you to develop them — and
maybe yourself a little, too — to make great things happen.

I CAN HELP.

My **event speaking, leadership coaching,** and **training**
will show you and your team how to unleash your real
power and take on any challenge as a unified front.

If you want to get past your roadblocks and have a little
fun along the path to success, let's talk. Schedule your free
initial consultation at:

www.indiebollman.com/contact

BONUS: *If you've read my book, you'll receive a discount off
your first contract (depending on package selected) if you sign
within 30 days of your consultation. There's your first win-win!*